MAKE A JOYFUL NOISEMAKER

Mark Burrows

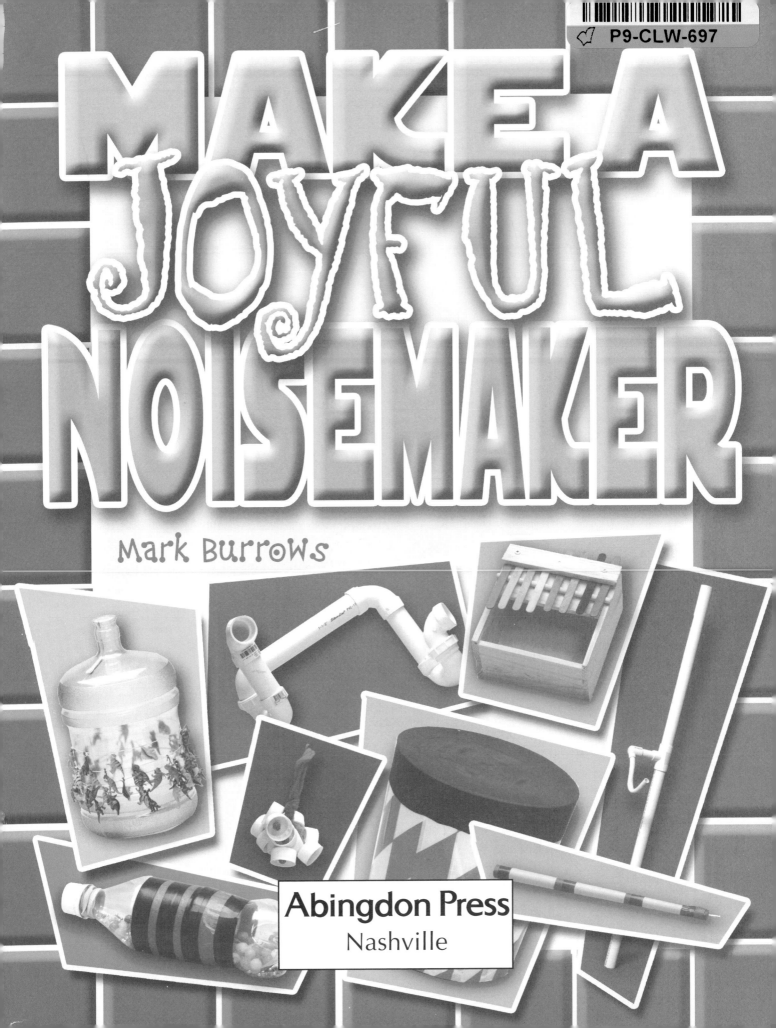

Abingdon Press

Nashville

Make a Joyful Noisemaker

ISBN 0-687-49346-3

Writer: Mark Burrows
Photos by: Ron Benedict
Editor: LeeDell Stickler
Production Editor: Alex Petrounov
Production and Design Manager: R.E. Osborne
Designer: cover, Paige Easter; interior, Gillian Housewright

06 07 08 09 10 11 12 13 14 15—10 9 8 7 6 5 4 3 2 1

ACKNOWLEDGEMENTS

I would like to thank the following people whose support and encouragement through the years have blessed my life and my work.

Larry Beman, Barbara Bruce, Bethany Buchholtz, Sandra Carter, Cathy Hoop, Sandy Mabry, Cynthia McElrath, Linda Ray Miller, Gary Alan Smith, Patti Anderson Smith, LeeDell Stickler, Carol Szabo, Debi Tyree, Suzann Wade, Sally Wizik-Wills, and, of course my three girls, Nina, Emma, and Grace.

This book is dedicated to Daphna Flegal.

CONTENTS

Making Instruments—Making Choices 6

Integrating Instrument Making Into a Lesson 7

The Original Noisemaker—The Body 8

Mouth Music—More Than Singing 11

Let's Make Some Noisemakers 13

    Soda Bottle Shofar 14

    Clickin' Castanets 15

    The Sistrum 16

    Makin' Waves With Ocean Drums 17

    Rockin' Rainsticks 18

    The Guiro 20

    A Symphony of Sounds From a Soda Bottle 21

    Soda Bottle Maracas 22

    Clip Clop Hooves 23

    Chajchas 24

    Miscellaneous Instruments 25

    A Soda Bottle Symphony 26

    Go, Go Agogo Bells 27

    What's Shaking With Shakeres? 29

    The Shake-O-Saurus 31

    Make a Peck of Panpipes 32

    A Little Balloon Music, Please 34

    Peter Yes-and-No Drum 35

    Amazing Tone Tubes 38

    The Cuica 41

    Didgeridoo 43

    Slide Didgeridoo 45

    Nessie 46

    The Bull-Roarer 47

    The Kalimba 49

    The Kazooka 51

Drums, Drums, and More Drums 53

    A Small Hand Drum 54

    Bingo, Bango, Bongos 55

    The Doumbek 57

    The Tambourine 59

Stringed Instruments 61
The Harp 61
The Berimbau 63
The Dollar Store Djembe 65
Effective Sound Effects 67
One String Guitar 70
Some Simple Gifts 71

Let's Make Some Joyful Noise 72
Making Music in the Classroom 73
Rhythmic Passing Games 74
Percussion Jams 76
Create a Tone Poem 78
Incidental Music 80
Compose a Soundtrack 84
Call and Response 86
Accompany a Bible Song 88
Create a Musical Sound Effects Story 89
A Story With a Beat 90

Some Helpful Things (Reproducibles) 92
Bull-Roarer Pattern 93
Harp Pattern 94
Tone Tube Sheets:
    "Joyful, Joyful, We Adore Thee" 95
    "Amazing Grace" 96
    "Away in a Manger" 97
    "For the Beauty of the Earth" 98
The Sound of Symbols 99
Rhythm of Respect 99
Percussion Jam 100
Communion Drum Circle 101
Holy Spirit 102
A Story With a Beat 103
The Ten Commandments 104
Conservation Concert 105
Story Samba 106
Go Fish 107
Percussion With Proverbs 108

Index 109

MAKING INSTRUMENTS—MAKING CHOICES

When the editors at Abingdon Press asked me to create a resource for making musical instruments, I knew it would be fun. What I didn't anticipate was how challenging it would be. And the biggest challenge was in choosing what to put in, and what to leave out.

Here are some of the things I considered when making those choices:

1. Cost. Most of us work with several kiddos each week. I wanted to make sure that each instrument was relatively inexpensive to make.

2. I left out the most obvious instruments. We all know how to make a rattle out of a jar and some beads, or a drum out of a coffee can. I tried to include instruments that might not be as obvious, such as the coffee can cuica or the shekere.

3. Child involvement. Most of the instruments in this resource require at least some prep work by an adult. The trick is to make sure the children still have ownership of the project. The children should feel as if they are the ones making the instrument, not just helping some adult.

4. Safety. There are books full of ideas for making your own musical instruments. Some of these instruments are fantastic, but require the use of tools that simply aren't age-appropriate. Any instrument project in this resource that requires sawing, drilling, and so forth strongly suggests that this step be done by an adult.

5. No food in arts and crafts. Years ago, when I first started writing for Abingdon, I learned that they do not recommend the use of food for art and craft projects in a hungry world. My initial thought was, "Okay, that's noble and all, but is it really practical? What about all those macaroni necklaces? And dried corn makes such a great sound for rattles and rain sticks." One handful of dried corn in one rattle may not be a big deal. But imagine that one hundred people buy this book (a lofty goal, but hey, I'm a dreamer). If each of these people completes the art and craft projects with the use of food, there will be a lot of wasted food!

INTEGRATING INSTRUMENT MAKING INTO A LESSON

MAKE A JOYFUL NOISEMAKER is full of practical suggestions for making fun musical instruments. The instruments you choose to make will depend on what you're trying to teach.

- Make the instrument fit the story.
  If you're teaching children about David, the boy, the harp is a natural fit. An ocean drum makes a fine complement to a lesson on Jonah. You can enhance a lesson on Noah by making rain sticks. Musical instruments of different cultures can add excitement when exploring Christmas around the world. Virtually any instrument can add to a lesson on the psalms.

- Consider making more than one.
  Many of the instruments are time-friendly enough to make that the children can make more than one instrument per lesson. But this is not always the case.

- Create an instrumentarium.
  In any given instrument-making activity, some children will simply finish well before others. Challenge these children to make another of the same instrument that may be kept in the music station. Then, when an activity requires a wide variety of musical instruments, you will have a fine collection from which to choose.

- Make use of recyclable materials.
  Most of the instruments and noisemakers in this resource call for the use of recyclable materials. Don't feel like you have to collect 120 cardboard tubes or 80 plastic soda bottles on your own. Provide a few large bins in the music station, and have the children bring the materials from home.

- Plan in advance.
  If you are going to have the children make tone tubes, you will need a lot of long cardboard tubes. When is the best time of year to collect a lot of cardboard tubes? Christmas, of course! Have the kids be on the lookout at home for empty wrapping paper tubes and bring them in. By February or March, you should have more cardboard tubes than you know what to do with.

- Purchase only the essentials.
  Always keep a stock of colored electrical and masking tapes, available at any hardware store.

A SAMPLE LIST:

1. Stomp
2. Clap
3. Snap
4. Patschen (patting the thighs)
5. Tongue clicks
6. Rub hands together for friction sound
7. Lightly thump cheek while mouth is open
8. Click heels together
9. Pat chest
10. Pat stomach

I praise you, for I am fearfully and wonderfully made.
Psalm 139:14

The body was not only the first musical instrument, but in many cultures it is still the instrument of choice. Many Native American and African cultures incorporate rhythmic stomping into certain ceremonies. Spanish flamenco music is often accompanied by very intricate clapping patterns. Fa' ataupati, a traditional Samoan dance, involves men slapping their torsos, arms, and legs. And who can imagine jazz without that snapping on the downbeat?

And that's just the body as a percussion instrument. What about all the sound possibilities of the human voice? Aside from singing, we have whistling, buzzing, humming, yodeling, tongue clicks, and much more. The human body is nothing short of a walking, breathing orchestra!

EXPLORING BODY PERCUSSION

Have the children sit with you on the floor in a circle. Give them a few minutes to explore all the percussive sounds they can make using their bodies. Remind them to use their own bodies, not their neighbors'.

Next, allow the children to share the sounds they discovered. Ask for a volunteer to demonstrate a body percussion sound he or she found. Have the others imitate that sound. Allow each child a chance to demonstrate a body percussion sound.

If a chalkboard or dry-erase board is available, make a written list of all the different body percussion sounds demonstrated.

Not only are these different sounds, but each individual sound will also vary from child to child. No two well-crafted instruments (and there is no doubt that we are well-crafted instruments) ever sound exactly alike.

TELL A BIBLE STORY USING BODY PERCUSSION

Read the following Bible story from Luke 19 to the children.

[Jesus] entered Jericho and was passing through it.

A man was there named Zacchaeus; he was a chief tax collector and was rich.

He was trying to see who Jesus was, but on account of the crowd he could not, because he was short in stature.

So he ran ahead and climbed a sycamore tree to see Jesus, because he was going to pass that way.

When Jesus came to the place, he looked up and said to him, "Zacchaeus, hurry and come down; for I must stay at your house today."

So he hurried down and was happy to welcome him.

All who saw it began to grumble and said, "[Jesus] has gone to be the guest of one who is a sinner."

Zacchaeus stood there and said to the Lord, "Look, half of my possessions, Lord, I will give to the poor; and if I have defrauded anyone of anything, I will pay back four times as much."

Then Jesus said to him, "Today salvation has come to this house, because he too is a son of Abraham. For the Son of Man came to seek out and to save the lost."

This is a familiar story, and a favorite of many children. Any child who has been to a parade can certainly sympathize with Zacchaeus' difficulty in seeing what's going on. From a musical standpoint this story is great because there is a lot of action: Jesus entered Jericho; Zacchaeus ran ahead; the crowd began to grumble. Even the locations of the action have musical potential: Zacchaeus climbs up a sycamore tree, then hurries down the tree.

Read the story again, this time challenging the children to listen with their "musical ears." Have them identify actions, places, quotes, descriptions, and even people that could be depicted using body percussion.

After reading the story ask for children to suggest body percussion sounds that may be performed in place of these actions, places, quotes, descriptions, and people.

Here are some examples.

- Jesus entering Jericho could be depicted by rubbing hands together to a slow, steady walking beat.
- Zacchaeus climbing up the tree could be depicted by a series of tongue clicks, each one getting higher.
- Zacchaeus hurrying down the tree could be depicted by a series of faster tongue clicks, each one getting lower.
- The grumbling of the crowd could be depicted by shuffling feet.

Once the children have offered several suggestions, read the story to them a third time. This time have the children perform the suggested body percussion sounds where appropriate.

As a final step, have the children perform the body percussion sounds in sequence without reading them the story. Allow the sounds to tell the story.

This form of music, where instruments (in this case, the human body) are used to portray a story, scene, or, mood, is called a tone poem.

There are hundreds of biblical passages, from proverbs to parables, that could make great tone poems. The best are those that contain a lot of action.

MOUTH MUSIC—MORE THAN SINGING

O Lord, open my lips,
and my mouth will declare your praise.
Psalm 51:15

It's natural to think of singing when thinking about the sounds we make with our mouths and voices. But why should we feel so limited? There are so many sounds we can make with our mouths. Why not use them all?

EXPLORING MOUTH MUSIC

Invite the children to spend a few moments exploring the different sounds they can make with their voices and/or their mouths. Challenge them to do so without speaking or singing any actual words.

Next, allow each child a chance to share a sound he or she discovered. Have the others imitate that sound. If a chalkboard or dry-erase board is available, write down all the vocal or mouth sounds the children share.

The possibilities are virtually limitless.

USE THE VOICE TO CREATE A SOUND EXPERIENCE

Read the following traditional Gaelic rune, "Christ in the Stranger's Guise," to the children.

Christ in the Stranger's Guise
I met a stranger yest're'en;
I put food in the eating place,
Drink in the drinking place,
Music in the list'ning place,
And in the name of the Triune,
He blessed myself and my house,
My cattle,
And my loved ones.
And the lark sang in his song,
"Often goes the Christ in the stranger's guise."

This rune is as poetic as it is prayerful, offering many opportunities for musical expression.

A SAMPLE LIST:
1. whistle
2. hum
3. buzz
4. bubble the lips
5. tongue clicks
6. pop lips like a fish
7. hiss
8. sigh
9. laugh
10. gulp
11. roar
12. growl
13. howl
14. blow to make a wind sound

Read it again, this time having the children offer vocal or mouth sounds that can be made after each line is read, or in place of each line. For example:

TEXT	VOCAL SOUND
I met a stranger yest're'en;	wind sounds
I put food in the eating place,	smacking or "mmm" sounds
Drink in the drinking place,	gulping sounds
Music in the listening place,	hum or imitate an instrument
And in the name of the Triune, He blessed myself and my house,	hammering and sawing sounds
My cattle	mooing sounds
And my loved ones.	warm sighing sounds
And the lark sang in his song,	whistling sounds
"Often goes the Christ in the stranger's guise."	wind sounds

LET'S MAKE SOME NOISEMAKERS

SODA BOTTLE SHOFAR

WHAT YOU'LL NEED:

- empty, clean, plastic soda bottles
- colored masking tape
- colored electrical tape
- hacksaw
- scissors

So David and all the house of Israel brought up the ark of the LORD with shouting, and with the sound of the trumpet.
2 Samuel 6:15

The shofar is a trumpet made from a ram's horn. It is used in modern Jewish worship for Rosh Hashanah and Yom Kippur.

BEFORE THE KIDDOS ARRIVE

Make sure to wash the plastic soda bottles thoroughly. Use a hacksaw to cut off the bottom of each bottle. Use electrical tape to seal the newly cut edge of each bottle.

MAKE THE SHOFAR

Give each child one plastic bottle and a pair of scissors. Place several rolls of masking tape and electrical tape around the room.

Invite the children to decorate their bottles using the masking tape and electrical tape. Masking tape works very well for covering the surface of the bottle. The electrical tape can make rings or other patterns around the bottles.

Make sure the children leave both ends of the bottle uncovered.

SOUND THE SHOFAR

Playing the shofar is similar to playing a trumpet. Have the children buzz their lips. They can make the pitch lower by loosening their lips as they buzz. To make the pitch higher, have them tighten their lips as they buzz.

Next, have the children put their shofars gently to their lips as they continue to buzz. Invite the children to explore the different pitches they can make with their shofars.

CLICKIN' CASTANETS

David and all the house of Israel were dancing before the LORD with all their might, with songs and lyres and harps and tambourines and castanets and cymbals.
2 Samuel 6:5

- large plastic bottle caps (larger bottle caps work better than typical soda bottle caps)

- cardboard (2 inches by 6 inches)

- glue sticks or double-sided tape

- crayons or markers

- scissors

- ruler

We usually associate castanets with Spanish music rather than David. But there they are in Second Samuel.

The word *castanet* is derived from the Spanish *castanuela*, which means "chestnut." It's not hard to imagine the clicking of chestnut shells serving as the original castanets.

BEFORE THE KIDDOS ARRIVE

Wash and dry the bottle caps. Cut cardboard into two- by six-inch strips.

MAKE THE CASTANETS

Give each child a strip of cardboard. Allow the children to choose from the assorted crayons and markers and decorate one side of their cardboard strips.

Next, give each child two bottle caps and either a glue stick or two small pieces of double-sided tape. Have the children glue or tape the bottle caps flat side down to each end of the undecorated side of the cardboard strip. Have the children fold their cardboard strips in the middle so the bottle caps can touch.

If the children use glue sticks, set the castanets aside so the glue can dry. If the children use tape, then the castanets are ready for playing.

CLICK THE CASTANETS

Clicking the castanets is fun and easy. Place them lightly between the thumb and fingers and press down to click. If time allows, invite each child to make two sets of castanets, one for each hand. Have the children explore the different rhythms they can create with their castanets.

THE SISTRUM

All the trees of the field shall
clap their hands.
Isaiah 55:12b

WHAT YOU'LL NEED:

- Y-shaped sticks
- chenille stems
- metal washers of various sizes (but not too heavy)
- optional: sandpaper

The sistrum is an Egyptian rattle that was used in Bible times.

BEFORE THE KIDDOS ARRIVE

The biggest job is collecting all the Y-shaped sticks. It works best if the sticks are from 12 to 18 inches long. Once you have collected enough Y-shaped sticks, check each to make sure there are no rough edges or sharp points. Some light sanding may be required.

MAKE A SISTRUM

1. Give each child a Y-shaped stick, two chenille stems, and several assorted metal washers.
2. Have the children wrap a chenille stem three times around one prong of the Y-shaped stick.
3. Next, have them thread half of the washers over the loose end of the chenille stem.
4. Then have them wrap the loose end of the chenille stem tightly around the other prong of the Y-shaped stick.

Repeat this process with the other chenille stem and the remaining washers.

In some cases, the Y may not be big enough for two sets of chenille stems and washers. One set will work fine. Or, with a larger stick, use more than two. (See photo.)

JINGLE THE SISTRUM

Have the children shake their sistrums back and forth so that the washers run along the length of the chenille stems, clicking each other and the prongs of the Y-shaped stick.

MAKING WAVES WITH OCEAN DRUMS

And they said to one another, "Who then is this, that he commands even the winds and the water, and they obey him?"
Luke 8:25b, adapted

The ocean drum is a two-headed frame drum with small, round beads inside that, when rolled from side to side, produce a wavelike sound. The ocean drum has been found in many cultures from Nepal to the Mayans.

BEFORE THE KIDDOS ARRIVE

The ocean drum is one of the easiest instruments to make and requires no before-class preparation. If you cannot find pie pans with plastic lids, have the children put two pie pans together using tape or staples.

MAKE AN OCEAN DRUM

Give each child an aluminum pie plate, a plastic lid, and a handful of plastic beads. Have each child place the beads in the pie plate and secure the plastic lid.

It's that easy! If you want to do more, have the children decorate their ocean drums. Give each child a paper circle (cut to the circumference of the bottom of the pie plate) and several crayons.

Invite the children to decorate their paper circles with scenes from whichever Bible story is being learned.

Have the children use glue sticks or double-sided tape to attach their pictures to the bottom inside of their drums. The clear plastic lids should allow the children to see their pictures as they play their drums.

PLAY THE OCEAN DRUM

Hold the drum horizontally and gently tilt it from side to side so that the beads roll across the bottom. Have the children experiment with the angles at which they tilt their drums. The steeper the angle, the bigger and louder the wave crash will be.

WHAT YOU'LL NEED:

- small, round plastic beads

- aluminum pie plates with clear plastic lids

- optional: extra aluminum pans, staples or tape, paper, scissors, crayons, glue sticks or double-sided tape

SOME BIBLE STORIES THAT INVOLVE WATER

- Jonah (Jonah 1:1–15)

- Jesus calms the storm (Luke 8:22–25)

- Noah (Genesis 7:17–20)

- Paul Sails to Rome (Acts 27)

17

ROCKIN' RAINSTICKS

WHAT YOU'LL NEED:

- long cardboard tubes (wrapping paper tubes work best)

- straight pins

- small plastic beads

- clear book tape or packaging tape

- funnel or measuring cup

- construction paper, printer paper, stickers, colored masking tape

Ask rain from the LORD in the season of the spring rain, from the LORD who makes the storm clouds, who gives showers of rain to you, the vegetation in the field to everyone.
Zechariah 10:1

The rainstick is of South American origin. It is traditionally made from a hollowed-out cactus stem with the needles of the cactus pushed into the center of the stem. Small pebbles, dried corn, or crushed seashells are placed inside the stem, where they trickle down over the cactus needles, causing a gentle, rain-like sound.

BEFORE THE KIDDOS ARRIVE

Straight pins are a big challenge for little fingers. If you decide to make rainsticks with younger children, I highly recommend that you use pins with ball heads and shorter cardboard tubes. Alternative: Press the pins in ahead of time.

MAKE A RAINSTICK

Give each child a cardboard tube and a container of straight pins. Remind the children to be careful and take their time handling the pins.

Instruct the children to push pins into the side of their tubes. Make sure the children press the pins the whole length of the tube, as well as all around the tube. The more pins there are in the tube, the more the final instrument will sound like rain when played. For this reason, it is a good idea to allow plenty of time for this step.

Next, give each child a piece of tape wide enough to seal one end of his or her tube. Use the clear packing tape to cover the tube and secure the straight pins.

Give each child one to two handfuls (about 1/4 to 1/2 cup) of small plastic beads. Use a funnel or a measuring cup to pour the beads into each tube.

Have the children seal the other end of the remaining open end of the tube.

Give the children one of the following options on how to cover the rainstick:

- Cover the tube with wrapping paper. Tape or glue in place.

- Cover the tube with construction paper. Tape or glue in place.

- Cover the tube with brightly colored printer paper.

This covering not only decorates the rainstick, but it also keeps the pins in the tube.

COOL OPTION:
Let the children decorate the outside of their rainstick with stickers or cut-outs from contrasting colors.

MAKE RAIN
Have the children turn their rainsticks over and listen as the beads trickle over the pins, creating a rain sound. Invite the children to turn their rainsticks at different angles to change the sound.

SUGGESTED BIBLE STORIES

- Genesis 1:1–31 (Creation)

- Genesis 7:1–8:22 (Noah)

- 1 Kings 17–18 (Contest on Mt. Carmel)

- Psalm 147

- Matthew 7:24–29 (The House on the Rocks)

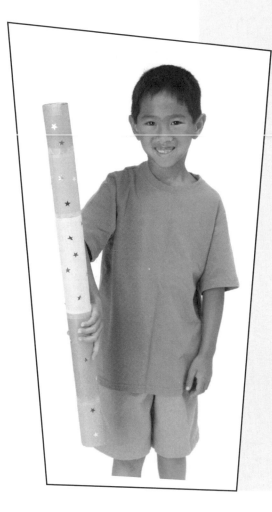

THE GUIRO

O come, let us sing to the Lord; let us make a joyful noise to the rock of our salvation!
Psalm 95:1

WHAT YOU'LL NEED:

- cardboard paper towel tubes
- roll of ribbed shelf liner
- ribbon in assorted colors
- scissors
- unsharpened pencils
- colored rubber bands

The guiro (pronounced WEE-roh) is a Latin American percussion instrument. Originally, the guiro was made from a dried, hollow gourd with notches cut into it. The notches are scraped with a stick.

BEFORE THE KIDDOS ARRIVE

Precut pieces of the ribbed shelf liner to fit around the cardboard tubes.

MAKE A GUIRO

Give each child a cardboard tube, a length of ribbed shelf liner, and three rubber bands. Have the children wrap the ribbed shelf liner around the cardboard tubes and secure in place using the rubber bands.

Next, allow the children to choose from an assortment of colored ribbon and cut two lengths (no more than ten inches each). Have the children tie a length of ribbon around each end of their tubes.

SCRAPE THE GUIRO

Give each child an unsharpened pencil. Have the children hold their guiros with one hand and scrape their pencils along the ridges. Invite the children to experiment with long and short strokes as well as up and down strokes. Have them listen to how the sound changes depending on how they scrape.

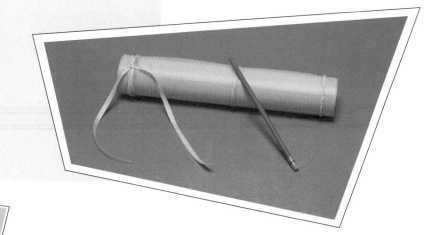

A SYMPHONY OF SOUNDS
FROM A SODA BOTTLE

Jesus said to them, "Have you never read in the scriptures: 'The stone that the builders rejected has become the cornerstone; this was the Lord's doing, and it is amazing in our eyes'?"
Matthew 21:42

We've heard about the resourcefulness of the Plains Indians—how they used every part of the bison, not just the meat. The hide was used for clothing and shelter. The bones were used for tools. This was not only resourceful, but also very respectful of the environment. I've always been fascinated and inspired by that way of life. Perhaps that's why I enjoy making musical instruments out of materials that might otherwise be thrown away.

Take the average twenty-ounce soda bottle. We could drink the soda and toss the empty bottle in the garbage (or recycling bin). Or we could see it for all the sound-making possibilities it holds. You'd be surprised at just how many there are. In the next few pages are some of those possibilities.

SODA BOTTLE MARACAS

Maracas are some of the easiest instruments to make using soda bottles.

WHAT YOU'LL NEED:

- empty, clean soda bottles with caps
- small plastic beads, variety of shapes and sizes
- colored masking tape
- scissors

BEFORE THE KIDDOS ARRIVE

Make sure to wash and dry all the soda bottles.

MAKE MARACAS

Give each child a soda bottle and a handful of beads. Have the children place the beads inside their bottles and secure the bottle caps. Next, invite them to decorate the outside of their bottles using the colored masking tape. (Masking tape is wonderful for covering rounded surfaces.)

PLAY THE MARACAS

Have the children hold their maracas with the capped end facing the floor, and shake them in a back-and-forth motion. Next, have them hold their maracas with the bottom of the bottles facing the floor and make swirling motions to produce a totally different sound.

CLIP-CLOP HOOVES

If you've already made shofars, don't throw away the bottoms of the bottles. They make excellent sound effects instruments.

BEFORE THE KIDDOS ARRIVE

Remove the bottoms of plastic soda bottles using a utlity knife. For younger children it may be advisable to seal the cut edges of the bottles using electrical tape.

MAKE CLIP-CLOP HOOVES

Give each child the bottoms of two plastic bottles. (When you vary the size, you vary the sound.) Have each child use electrical tape to cover the cut edges of the bottles.

PLAY THE CLIP-CLOP HOOVES

Have the children use a hard flat surface, such as a table or desk, on which to tap the open ends of the clip-clop hooves. Have them try to represent different speeds such as a slow donkey or a galloping steed. The hooves can even be the plodding footsteps of God's people in the wilderness.

Don't limit the Clip-Clop Hooves only to donkeys. This will only limit the number of Bible stories. Think of the other hooved animals in the Bible: camels, oxen, sheep, goats, and even pigs. These can even be used for footsteps in traveling Bible stories. See the list of possible stories to your right. But don't let these limit you. Use your imagination.

WHAT YOU'LL NEED:

- bottoms of plastic bottles

- utility knife

- electrical tape

- scissors

SOME SUGGESTED BIBLE STORIES

- 1 Samuel 3:1–21 (The Call of Samuel)

- 1 Samuel 25:2–35 (David and Abigail)

- Luke 2:1–7 (The Journey to Bethlehem)

- Matthew 2:1–2 (The Journey of the Magi)

- Luke 15:11–32 (The Forgiving Father)

- Luke 19:28–40 (Palm Sunday)

CHAJCHAS

The chajchas is an Andean rattle made by stringing together goat toes. Not to worry, the goats shed their hooves naturally. Similar rattles are made in Africa by stringing together dried nut shells or seed pods. We can create a similar sound and no animal (or plant) be bothered.

BEFORE THE KIDDOS ARRIVE

(Adults or older children only) Use a hammer and a nail to punch holes in the top of each bottle cap. (Vary the color of the bottle caps and beads just for fun. The sound will be the same but the color adds interest.)

MAKE THE CHAJCHAS

Give each child six to ten bottle caps, one approximately three-foot length of yarn, scissors, and six to ten beads. Make sure the beads are large enough that when added to the end of the yarn will prevent the bead from pulling through the nail hole.

Have each child cut yarn into eight-inch lengths (one strand for every two bottle caps).

Have each child thread a strand of yarn through a bottle cap (from the top side to the inside) and tie a bead to the end of the strand. This will keep the yarn from slipping back through the hole in the bottle cap.

Next, have each child thread the other end of the strand of yarn through another bottle cap and tie a bead to that end.

Allow the children to continue until each of their strands has a bottle cap attached to both ends.

Have the children tie the strands of yarn together in the middle, leaving the bottle caps loose enough to rattle together when shaken.

PLAY THE CHAJCHAS

Have the children hold their chajchas by the yarn handle and bounce them in short up-and-down motions.

Another option is to hold the chajchas with one hand and tap the caps into the other hand.

WHAT YOU'LL NEED:

- clean, plastic bottle caps (six to ten per child)

- yarn

- scissors

- beads

- hammer

- nail

MISCELLANEOUS INSTRUMENTS

BOTTLE MALLETS

Take the caps off two plastic soda bottles and play them against a flat surface such as the floor. Let the children decorate them with colored masking tape or colored electrical tape.

CRICKETS

Most soda bottle caps are ridged on the outside. Take two caps and rub the edges together, creating a friction sound not unlike a cricket.

BOTTLE FLUTE

Take the cap off an empty soda bottle and blow across the opening as you would a flute.

Have the children experiment with high and low sounds by adding different levels of water to their bottles. The more water—the higher the pitch. The less water—the lower the pitch. Adding more water decreases the air mass in the bottle, which is being vibrated when you blow across the top of the bottle.

WHAT YOU'LL NEED:

• soda bottles

• soda bottle caps

• water

A SODA BOTTLE SYMPHONY

Have the children use these soda bottle instruments (see pages 21—25) to play the Soda Bottle Symphony as you, or another child, narrate.

WHAT YOU'LL NEED

- soda bottle mallets

- soda bottle clip clop hooves

- soda bottle shofar

- soda bottle flutes

- bottle cap chajchas

- soda bottle maracas

OTHER SUGGESTED BIBLE STORIES

- The Stories of Holy Week (Suggested break-down of stories you could use)
  Palm Sunday
  Cleansing the Temple
  The Last Supper
  Praying in the Garden
  Jesus' Arrest
  Jesus' Trial
  Jesus' Crucifixion
  Jesus' Resurrection

MOVEMENT 1—JOURNEY TO BETHLEHEM

In those days a decree went out from Emperor Augustus (*Soda bottle mallets play a drum roll.*) that all the world would be registered. All went from their own towns to be registered. Joseph went from the town of Nazareth in Galilee to Judea, to the City of David called Bethlehem, because he was descended from the family of David.

(*Soda bottle hooves play clippity-clop.*) He went to be registered with Mary, to whom he was engaged, and who was expecting a child. While they were there, the time came for her to deliver her child. She wrapped her son in bands of cloth, and laid him in a manger, (*Soda bottle shofar plays cow sounds.*) because there was no place for them in the inn.

MOVEMENT 2—SHEPHERDS AND ANGELS

(*Blow across the tops of the soda bottle flutes to make wind sounds. Make soda bottle cricket sounds as well.*) In that region there were shepherds in the fields, keeping watch over their flock by night. (*Bottle cap chajchas play for sheep steps.*) Then an angel of the Lord stood before them, and the glory of the Lord shone around them, and they were terrified. But the angel said to them, "Do not be afraid; for see—I am bringing you good news of great joy for all people: to you is born this day in the City of David a Savior, who is the Messiah, the Lord. This will be a sign to you: you will find a child wrapped in bands of cloth and lying in a manger."

And suddenly there was with the angel a multitude of the heavenly host, praising God and saying, (*Soda bottle shofars play trumpet herald.*) "Glory to God in the highest heaven, and on earth peace to all!" When the angels left, the shepherds went in haste to Bethlehem, (*Soda bottle maracas play hurrying sounds.*) and found Mary, Joseph, and the child lying in the manger. When they saw this, they made known what had been told them about this child; and all who heard it were amazed at what the shepherds told them. But Mary treasured all these words and pondered them in her heart. The shepherds returned, glorifying and praising God for all they had heard and seen. (*Play all the soda bottle instruments together.*)

GO, GO, AGOGO BELLS

*They also made bells of pure gold,
and put the bells between the pomegranates
on the lower hem of the robe all around.*
Exodus 39:25

Okay, so you probably don't have a lot of pure gold just lying around. You can still make a cool instrument. Agogo bells are a set of two bells, one with a higher pitch, and one with a lower pitch. They are used in the samba music of Brazil.

BEFORE THE KIDDOS ARRIVE

Make sure the bottles are clean. Since this instrument involves screws and screwdrivers, it is best to do this activity with older children.

MAKE AGOGO BELLS

Divide the children into small groups. Give each child two soft plastic baby bottles and a wooden spoon.

Give each group a few rolls of colored electrical tape and scissors. Go to each of the small groups and help them attach the bottles to the wooden spoon.

Use the screwdriver to drive the screw through the smaller bottle. The screw should come out of the bottom of the bottle.

Drive the screw through the wooden spoon. Then drive the screw through the long bottle so that the pointed end is inside the bottle.

Note: Because of the use of screws in this instrument, it may work best for you to do the assembly work. By dividing the children into small groups, you can more easily assemble the instruments for one group while the other groups use the electrical tape to decorate the handles of their spoons.

Remember to have the pointed end of the screw go through the longer bottle. That makes it virtually impossible for any little fingers to get accidentally poked.

WHAT YOU'LL NEED:

- soft plastic baby bottles of different sizes (two bottles per child)

- wooden spoons (one per child)

- screws

- screwdrivers

- unsharpened pencils (one per child)

- colored electrical tape

- scissors

PLAY THE AGOGO BELLS

Give each child an unsharpened pencil. (If you wait until all the instruments are assembled before you pass out the pencils, you will decrease the noise level while you're helping to assemble the agogo bells.)

Invite the children to tap the bells with their pencils. The children can also tap the bells on the table.

Allow them the opportunity to experiment with different patterns of pitch and rhythm.

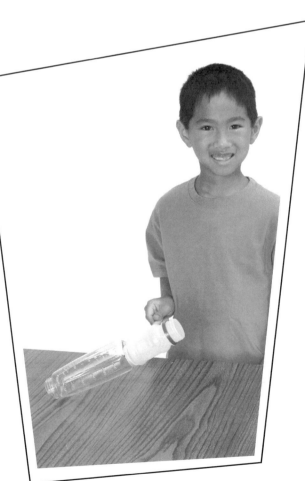

WHAT'S SHAKIN' WITH SHAKERES?

For you, O LORD, have made me glad by your work; at the works of your hands I sing for joy.
Psalm 92:4

The shekere (SHEH keh reh) is a rattle-like instrument of African origin that is also popular in Latin American music. Originally a shekere was made from a dried gourd wrapped in a net of beads or shells.

BEFORE THE KIDDOS ARRIVE

Wash the plastic sports drink bottles. Sports drink bottles work better than soda bottles since they tend to be larger, with larger openings.

Cut several lengths of thread (one for each bottle). If you are using large plastic bottles, lengths of at least three feet should be cut. If the bottles are small, lengths of about two feet should be enough. Just remember to cut a little on the long side. It's easier to cut some excess thread than it is to add more.

MAKE A SHEKERE

Give each child a bottle, a thirty-six inch length of thread, and two rubber bands. (Use colorful rubber bands that are available at most office supply stores.)

Have each child wrap one rubber band around the base of the bottle and the other rubber band around the neck of the bottle.

Next, have each child tie one end of the thread to the rubber band at the base of the bottle. Leave about a four-inch tail for attaching the other end once the children have gone all around the bottle.

Place several containers of beads around the room. Have the children choose the beads they would like to use for their instruments.

Invite each child to string several beads on the thread; then tuck the thread under the rubber band at the neck of the bottle and pull the thread through.

WHAT YOU'LL NEED:

- empty, plastic sports drink bottles

- rubber bands

- sturdy cotton crochet thread (available at most craft stores)

- wooden or plastic beads

- scissors

- optional: fishing line

Make sure the thread is not too tight, or the beads will not be able to slap against the side of the bottle.

Have each child string more beads onto the thread and pull the thread under the rubber band at the base of the bottle. Continue in a zigzag pattern as shown here. The more beaded strands, the more noise.

When the zigzag pattern reaches the point where the thread was first tied to the rubber band, have each child tie the other end as close as possible to the first knot. Tie securely.

Cut off any excess thread.

When making shekeres with younger children, remember that many of them will not have fully developed fine motor skills. The best way to modify this activity is to modify the materials.

- Use smaller bottles so that the children will not have to cover such a large surface area with beads.
- Use larger beads so that fewer beads will be needed.
- Choose beads with large holes for ease of threading.
- Sturdy fishing line makes an excellent substitute for thread, since it doesn't fray. But it is more difficult to tie.

SHAKE A SHEKERE

While the name shekere would imply that this instrument is to be shaken, there are actually many ways to make sounds with a shekere.

1. You can hold the shekere by the neck and base and shake it toward and away from your body.
2. You can tap the beads with your fingertips.
3. You can hold the neck with one hand and pat the base with the other.

Allow the children to experiment with different sounds. Invite them to listen to how every shekere sounds a little different. Plastic beads sound different than wooden beads. Big bottles sound different than little bottles. Big beads sound different than small beads.

THE SHAKE-O-SAURUS

Speaking of big bottles. . .

A really fun instrument to make is the Shake-o-saurus.

The shake-o-saurus is built like a shekere, with a few exceptions. Instead of a sports drink bottle, use a five-gallon water bottle. And instead of using beads, thread the entire bottle with small plastic dinosaurs!

Originally I wanted to make a giant shekere using pop-it beads. (Do you remember pop-it beads? They were big plastic beads that you could snap together.) Well, I looked all over, and it turns out that pop-it beads are hard to come by. Maybe impossible.

So I was in a toy store looking for them (or a possible substitute) when I happened by a shelf with plastic dinosaurs.

I thought to myself, "Why not? It could be fun."

That's how the very first Shake-o-saurus came to be. I took it to church one Sunday, and the kids went nuts over it.

Since the bottles are so big, (and plastic dinosaurs are generally more expensive than beads), this makes a great group activity. Take turns playing the Shake-O-Saurus.

Since most plastic dinosaurs don't come with pre-drilled holes, Cut the thread into three and four inch lengths. Tie each piece around a dinosaur's neck (or tail or leg) and then tie it to the sturdy thread.

Option: Tie the sturdy thread around each dinosaur in turn before threading it under the rubber bands.

WHAT YOU'LL NEED:

- five-gallon water bottle

- small plastic dinosaurs (or other plastic animals)

- sturdy cotton crochet thread or fishing line

- large rubber bands

MAKE A PECK OF PANPIPES

His brother's name was Jubal; he was the ancestor
of all those who play the lyre and pipe.
Genesis 4:21

WHAT YOU'LL NEED:

- ruler
- several straws for each child
- scissors
- rulers
- packing tape
- yarn
- plastic clay

Simple flutes made from hollowed-out pieces of cane were common in Bible times. Sometimes several cane pieces were laced together to make an instrument called pipes. Each pipe made a different sound, depending on its length. Panpipes are found all over the world and are still played today, most notably in Andean music.

BEFORE THE KIDDOS ARRIVE

You will not need to do any preparation for the older children. Younger children, however, may have a difficult time measuring and cutting each of the straws to the proper length. Pre-cut the straws to the suggested lengths for the younger children.

It is now possible to get packages of straws in assorted colors. If each length is represented by a different-colored straw, it will make the activity easier.

By the way, this book has many activities for using recycled materials. Do not, however, use recycled straws. (Gross!)

To save time for all ages, cut the yarn into 28-inch lengths (one for each child).

MAKE PANPIPES

Give each child eight straws, a pair of scissors, and a ruler. Have them cut the straws to the following lengths in inches:

1. 6 ¾	5. 4 ¼
2. 6	6. 3 ¾
3. 5 ¼	7. 3 ½
4. 4 ¾	8. 3 ¼

These are approximate lengths. Small variances, such as the thickness of the straws, can slightly alter the pitch. Err on the side of too long. You can always cut more off.

Give each child some plastic clay. Instruct the children to tear off eight small pieces and roll them into pea-sized balls. Then have them plug one end of each straw with the balls of plastic clay. It is better to have the children plug the holes at the ends that they cut, leaving the uncut ends open for playing. The ends the children cut tend to be more jagged than the uncut ends. Also, have the children take care not to push the plastic clay too far into the tubes, as that will alter the pitch.

Next, give each child a 9- to 10-inch piece of packing tape.

Have the children center the straws on the tape, side by side, from shortest to longest, with the open ends of the straws lined up evenly.

Have the children wrap the ends of the tape around the straws to hold them in place.

Give each child a length of yarn and two small pieces of tape. Have each child tape one end of the yarn to the end of the pipes with the longest tube and the other end of the yarn to the end of the pipes with the shortest tube.

Invite the children to wear the pipes around their necks.

PLAYING THE PANPIPES

Have the children hold the pipes vertically, then blow across the open ends. This will take some practice.

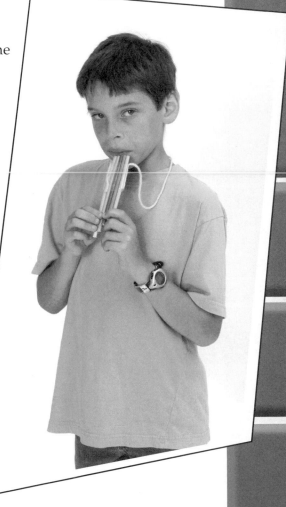

Ask the children to listen to the different sounds made by each of the individual pipes.

Invite them to create original melodies using their pipes.

By the way, don't throw away all those little straw pieces scattered around the room. You can use those to make little pocket-sized panpipes.

A LITTLE BALLOON MUSIC, PLEASE

WHAT YOU'LL NEED:

- balloons

- optional: sealable plastic bag, scissors

*When the day of Pentecost had come,
they were all together in one place.
And suddenly from heaven there came a sound
like the rush of a violent wind, and it filled
the entire house where they were sitting.
Acts 2:1-2*

I've always loved balloons and the sounds I could make with them. In fact, I remember going to the county fair and asking for a balloon that wasn't inflated. And yes, that got an odd look from the vendor, but think about all the sound possibilities!

You can:
1. Inflate the balloon, then let the air hiss out.
2. Inflate the balloon, then pull the opening tight so the air will squeak out.
3. Inflate the balloon, then tie it and tap it like a drum.
4. Inflate the balloon and tie it, then moisten your finger and rub along the side, creating a friction drum.
5. Pull an uninflated balloon tight and pluck.

Give each child a balloon. Invite the children to explore all the sound possibilities from one balloon.

Make sure to provide an option for any children allergic to latex. This can be a sealable plastic bag.

PETER YES-AND-NO DRUM

*When they had finished breakfast,
Jesus said to Simon Peter, "Simon son of John,
do you love me more than these?" He said to him,
"Yes, Lord; you know that I love you."
Jesus said to him, "Feed my lambs."
John 21:15*

WHAT YOU'LL NEED:

- sturdy paper plates, 6 inches in diameter (2 plates per child)

- paint stirrers (or wooden dowels)

- wooden beads

- yarn thin enough to be threaded through the beads or crochet thread

- stapler or clear tape

- scissors

- crayons or markers

The Peter Yes-and-No Drum is based on a spin drum also popularly known as a "monkey drum." The monkey drum is found in many world cultures and under many names, including damasas (Peru), duki duki (Zimbabwe), and kelontong (Java).

BEFORE THE KIDDOS ARRIVE

To save time, cut the yarn into 18-inch lengths.

MAKE A PETER YES-AND-NO DRUM

Give each child a paint stirrer and a length of yarn.

Have the children tie the yarn into a double knot around the paint stirrer, leaving two equal lengths of loose yarn.

Give each child two beads. Instruct the children to tie a bead to each loose end of yarn.

Next, give each child two paper plates. Have the children use the crayons to decorate a happy face on the back of one plate and a sad face on the back of the other.

Using clear tape (or duct tape), have the children attach the paint stirrer to the inside of one of the paper plates, decorated side facing out. The sad face should be vertical with the paint stirrer, and the happy face should be horizontal with the paint stirrer (unlike the photographs which are exactly backwards).

Make sure the beaded ends of the yarn are pulled out and perpendicular with the paint stirrer before attaching the plates.

SUGGESTED BIBLE STORIES

• Luke 22:54–62

PLAY THE PETER YES-AND-NO DRUM

Have the children hold their drums vertically and turn the stirrer back and forth. They should see the sad face shaking its head "no."

Have them turn their drums horizontally (make sure the happy face is right side up) and turn the stirrer back and forth. They should see the happy face nodding its head "yes."

PETER YES AND NO

Invite the children to use their Peter Yes-and-No Drums to play along as you read the story and the follow-up questions. Whenever the answer is "no," have the children play their drums vertically with the sad face toward the others. Whenever the answer is "yes," have the children play their drums horizontally, with the happy face toward the others.

PART 1:

One night Jesus and his disciples went to a garden of olive trees. Jesus prayed while the disciples slept. Soon an angry crowd arrived and took Jesus away.

The disciples ran away. Only Peter and one other remained. Peter followed at a safe distance to see where the crowd was taking Jesus. A woman saw Peter and asked, "Aren't you a follower of Jesus?"

Peter said, "No."

Another person recognized Peter and asked, "You are one of the disciples, aren't you?"

Again Peter said, "No."

A third person asked, "Didn't I see you in the garden with Jesus?"

Once again Peter responded, "No."

At that moment a rooster crowed.

Peter was very sad because he was afraid to admit he was a follower of Jesus. He thought he might never see Jesus again.

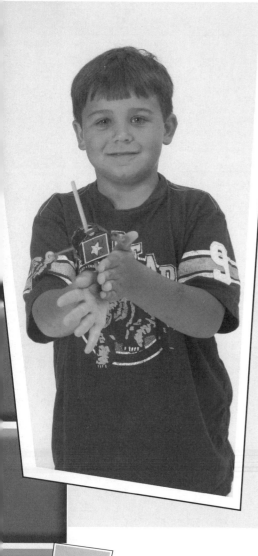

PART 2:

But many days later Peter did see Jesus and had breakfast with him on the beach.

Jesus asked Peter, "Do you love me?"

Peter answered, "Yes."

Jesus said, "Feed my lambs."

A second time Jesus asked Peter, "Do you love me?"

Peter answered, "Yes."

Jesus said, "Tend my sheep."

A third time Jesus asked Peter, "Do you love me?"

Peter said, "Yes."

Jesus said, "Feed my sheep."

Peter was happy because he was no longer afraid to admit how much he cared for Jesus. He knew Jesus would always be a part of his life.

QUESTIONS:

1. When people asked Peter if he was a disciple of Jesus, what did he say?
2. Is it always easy to follow Jesus?
3. Did Peter get a second chance to express his love for Jesus?

SUGGESTED BIBLE STORIES

• John 21:15–19

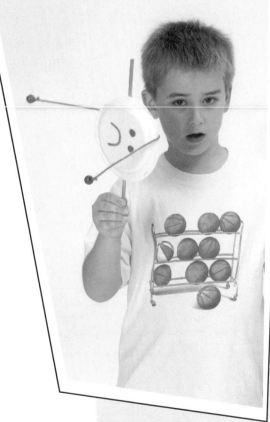

AMAZING TONE TUBES

My heart is steadfast, O God, my heart is steadfast. I will sing and make melody.
Psalm 57:7

WHAT YOU'LL NEED:

- cardboard tubes

- colored masking tape or electrical tape

- measuring tape or yardstick

- utility knife

- optional: plastic golf club tubes

What are tone tubes? Imagine taking the idea of panpipes, but about ten times bigger. And instead of blowing across the tops of the tubes, you tap them on a surface, such as a table, the floor, or the palm of your hand. There are fewer homemade instruments more fun to play than Tone Tubes.

BEFORE THE KIDDOS ARRIVE

For younger children cut the cardboard tubes to the suggested lengths below.

MAKE TONE TUBES

Give each child eight cardboard tubes, scissors, and a tape measure or yardstick.

Have the children measure and cut their tubes to the following lengths in inches:

Low C	24 5/8
D	21 7/8
E	19 3/8
F	18 1/8
G	16 1/8
A	14 1/2
Bb	13 3/8
High C	11 7/8

Why Bb instead of B? The measurements above are for tuning the tubes in F Major. Later on, when the children play songs with their tone tubes, the suggested tuning will work best with the arrangements included in this book. Incidentally, to make a B tube, cut it to 12 5/8 inches.

Give the children several rolls of electrical tape. Electrical tape comes in many colors now. Have the children decorate the tubes in the following colors:

Low C	red
D	yellow
E	purple
F	green
G	blue
A	black
Bb	orange
High C	white

If you notice, most cardboard tubes have a spiral seam that runs from end to end. Rather than covering each tube entirely with tape, have the children merely tape over the spiral seams. This accomplishes a couple of things. First, it gives each tube, and therefore each pitch, a different color without using nearly as much tape. Second, the tape, placed over the seams, will actually reinforce those seams, giving the tubes a longer playing life.

As with any homemade musical instrument that requires measuring and cutting for different pitches, cut on the long side. It is easier to go back and make another cut than start over with another tube. Remind the children not to rush the measuring process. I'm reminded of one of my engineering friends who always says, "Measure twice, cut once."

Cool Option: An alternative to cardboard tubes is using plastic golf club tubes. These can usually be purchased at a sporting goods store or the sporting goods section of a department store. The plastic is more difficult to cut, but it does make for a great-sounding tone tube.

You may wish to modify this activity by having a few small groups each make a set of tone tubes. While each child would not have a complete set of tubes to take home, each child would still have at least a couple of tubes to take home. And making only a few sets will move the process along more quickly so the children can get to do more playing.

PLAY THE TONE TUBES

Give each child a tone tube. Allow them to experiment with ways to play their tone tubes. They may tap the tubes in their hands, against their sides, on the floor, and so forth. Remind them that bonking their neighbors is not an option.

Contained in this book are several song arrangements for tone tubes (pages 95–98). The process is the same for each arrangement.

Give each child a tone tube sheet with the song to be played and several crayons.

Have the children color in the boxes using the colors indicated. At the bottom of each tone tube sheet is a color key.

Once the children have colored in all the boxes, assign each child one Tone Tube to correspond to the colored boxes. Every color will not always be used for every song, so make sure each child has a tube that will be used during that particular song.

Lead the children to play through the song. Have them follow along with the words and play whenever their tube corresponds to the colored box underneath the current word. Some boxes are long, and some boxes are short. The long boxes represent longer sounds, and the short boxes represent shorter sounds.

Occasionally a syllable will have two colored boxes underneath it, which means two notes are played for that syllable.

The arrangements in this book tend to be familiar, so if things fall apart, have the children sing through the song, then try again. You may even invite them to sing as they play, to help keep things together.

Following this process will allow children and adults to play songs without necessarily being able to read music.

THE CUICA

Wild animals and all cattle,
creeping things and flying birds!
Let them praise the name of the LORD.
Psalm 148:10, 13a

The cuica (KWEE kah) is a friction drum that is popular in the samba music of Brazil. The cuica has a stick in the center of the drum head, which is rubbed with a damp cloth. Many animal sounds can be imitated with the cuica.

BEFORE THE KIDDOS ARRIVE

If you are using old T-shirts, cut enough six-inch squares for each child to have one. It is best not to use squares cut from the armpits of the T-shirts. (Yuck!)

Use a can opener to open the bottom of each coffee can so that both ends are open.

CONSTRUCT A CUICA

Give each child a coffee can with a plastic lid, a bamboo skewer, two nuts, and two washers. Have each child thread one nut over the pointed end of the skewer to about one inch down the skewer.

Next, have each child place one washer over the pointed end of the skewer on top of the nut.

Have each child carefully push the pointed end of the skewer through the underside of the plastic lid until the lid is on top of the washer. (For safety, get a large block of plastic foam. Have the children place their plastic lid upside-down on the plastic foam and press the skewer through the lid. Hold the block in place while the children do this. This way they will not have to hold the lid with their free hand and risk getting poked.)

Have each child place the second washer on top of the lid and thread the second nut on top to hold the lid and washer securely in place.

Next, have the children attach the lids to their coffee cans and secure the lids with a few pieces of colored masking tape.

WHAT YOU'LL NEED

- old t-shirts, cut into six-inch squares
- scissors
- can opener
- large coffee can with plastic lid
- a bamboo skewer
- two nuts, same diameter as the bamboo skewer
- two washers, same diameter as the bamboo skewer
- block of plastic foam
- colored masking tape

Allow the children to decorate the outsides of their coffee cans using the colored masking tape.

PLAY THE CUICA

Give each child a damp cloth. Have the children rub the cloth along the skewers.

Invite them to experiment with their cuicas as they discover all the sound possibilities. A tight grip on the skewer will produce a different sound than a loose grip. A short stroke will produce a different sound than a long one. Pressing slightly on the lid with the free hand while playing will produce a different sound than not pressing the lid.

Have the children sit in a circle on the floor with their cuicas. Invite one child to imitate an animal sound with his or her cuica. The others must first guess which animal is being imitated. Then they must try to produce the same sound on their cuicas.

Allow each child a chance to imitate an animal sound on his or her cuica.

Read the following poem aloud. Invite the children to improvise sounds on their cuicas to accompany the text.

THE ARK WAS REALLY ROCKIN'

The ark was really rockin'.
It was quite a floating zoo.
The elephants and hippos
Were crammed in two-by-two.

The chimpanzees and monkeys
Would sing with all their might,
While pink flamingos danced along.
That ark was quite a sight.

The ark was filled up stem to stern,
With puppies, pigs, and skunks.
Oh sure, the ark was rockin',
But think how much it stunk!

DIDGERIDOO

The spirit of God has made me, and the breath of the Almighty gives me life.
Job 33:4

The didgeridoo (dih juh ree DOO) is an instrument found only in northern Australia. It is a wind instrument made from a long piece of bamboo or wood that is hollowed out. The player blows into one end while buzzing the lips, similar to playing a trumpet. The result is a low-pitched drone. The player may also hum, sing, or make other noises through the didgeridoo while playing, giving the instrument a wealth of sound possibilities.

There are many ways to make a didgeridoo. I'll show you some conventional and not-so-conventional ways to make your own. Choose the way that will work best in your learning environment.

BEFORE THE KIDDOS ARRIVE
The hardest part about a digeridoo is finding the cardboard tubes.

MAKE A CONVENTIONAL DIDGERIDOO
Give each child a cardboard tube and a few crayons. Invite the children to decorate their didgeridoos. You may suggest the children decorate their didgeridoos based on the story or concept being learned in Sunday school.

PLAY THE DIDGERIDOO
Have the children practice buzzing their lips. This is an unusual sensation, and actually makes the lips vibrate in a ticklish sort of way; ask any beginning trumpet player.

Then have the children hold one end of their didgeridoos to their buzzing lips.

They should press their lips tight enough to the openings that no air escapes from the sides of the mouth. But the pressure should be gentle to allow the buzzing to continue.

WHAT YOU'LL NEED

- cardboard tube
- crayons or markers

- plastic golf club tube

- scissors

- colored electrical tape

Allow the children time to experiment with the many sounds they can make with their didgeridoos. Have them try using:

1. more pressure on the opening
2. less pressure on the opening
3. tighter lips
4. looser lips
5. continuous droning
6. short rhythmic pulses
7. humming sounds as they buzz

Have the children do this kind of sound exploration, no matter how the didgeridoos are made.

CONVENTIONAL DIDGERIDOO 2

Give each child a plastic golf club tube, a pair of scissors, and a choice of colored electrical tape. Allow the children to decorate the tubes using the tape.

Use the same techniques with this instrument as you did the cardboard tubes.

SLIDE DIDGERIDOO

BEFORE THE KIDDOS ARRIVE

Remove the tops from all the mailing tubes. Then use the pliers to remove the caps from the bottoms of each tube. What you should have left is one longer tube that can slide back and forth inside a slightly shorter tube.

MAKE A SLIDE DIDGERIDOO

Give each child two mailing tubes, (two total tubes, one longer than the other), a PVC bushing, and a PVC elbow.

Have each child attach the elbow to one end of the longer cardboard tube.

Next, have each child connect the bushing to the elbow. This provides the mouthpiece.

Originally, the tree branch or bamboo stalk used for the didgeridoo would be too wide for players to buzz. So mouthpieces were often made out of beeswax. This gave the player a wide, resonant instrument with a narrow mouthpiece.

PLAY THE SLIDE DIDGERIDOO

Have the children hold the longer tube near the mouthpiece as they buzz into the didgeridoo. With their free hand have them slide the other tube up and down as they play. Ask them to observe how the sound changes depending on how long or short they make the instrument.

WHAT YOU'LL NEED

- mailing tubes
- pliers
- PVC bushings
- PVC elbows
- colored masking tape or electrical tape

45

NESSIE

WHAT YOU'LL NEED

- PVC pipes, various lengths

- assorted fittings, bushings

- hacksaw

- sandpaper

- disinfecting cloths

This is a special didgeridoo I like to call Nessie after that legendary Scottish animal. This instrument is a lot of fun to make.

BEFORE THE KIDDOS ARRIVE

Using the hacksaw, cut numerous lengths of pipe in a variety of lengths. Sand any rough edges.

MAKE NESSIE

Divide the children into small groups.

Give each group several lengths of pipe, an assortment of fittings, and enough bushings for each child to have one.

Allow the groups to build their own instruments in any shape or size they wish. Remind them that the bushings will serve as the mouthpiece.

PLAY NESSIE

Give each group ample time to try out many different combinations. Designate one child in each group to play their instrument for the other groups.

Avoid having three or four children use the same mouthpiece. Remind each child to use his or her own mouthpiece.

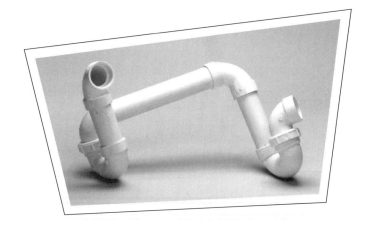

THE BULL-ROARER

*Then David took his staff in his hand,
and chose five smooth stones from the wadi,
and put them in his shepherd's bag, in the pouch;
his sling was in his hand, and he drew near
to the Philistine.*
1 Samuel 17:40, adapted

WHAT YOU'LL NEED:

- several pieces of corrugated cardboard

- several pairs of scissors

- sturdy string

- single-hole paper punches

- clear tape, assorted colors

- bull-roarer pattern (pg. 93)

- pencils

The bull-roarer is made by tying a long, flat piece of wood to a string. A roaring sound is produced by whirling the instrument overhead, similar to a sling.

BEFORE THE KIDDOS ARRIVE

Copy and cut out enough bull-roarer patterns (see page 93) so each child can have one.

MAKE A BULL-ROARER

Give each child a bull-roarer pattern and enough cardboard to trace and cut out two patterns.

Give the children pencils and have them trace the bull-roarer pattern twice.

Next, have the children cut out the patterns and punch holes where indicated on the pattern.

Have the children use clear tape to layer the two large pieces together into one thick piece. The holes in each piece should be aligned.

Follow the same steps for constructing the handle.

Have each child cut a piece of string about three feet long. Have the children tie one end of the string to the bull-roarer and the other end to the handle.

Allow the children to decorate their bull-roarers using the assorted colors of tape.

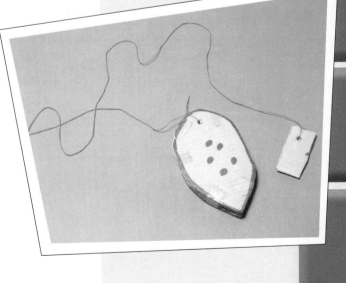

WHIRL THE BULL-ROARER

Obviously, this is an instrument that needs lots of space for playing. If you don't have a large enough space indoors, it's best to play the bull-roarer outside.

Have the children stand in a very wide circle.

Choose one child to stand in the center and whirl his or her bull-roarer overhead.

The thick piece of cardboard will start to turn on its own axis, causing a roaring sound.

It will take some practice to get the hang of it, but the plus side is that this activity will really wear out the kiddos!

THE KALIMBA

If the whole body were an eye, where would the hearing be? If the whole body were hearing, where would the sense of smell be? But as it is, God arranged the members in the body, each one of them, as he chose. If all were a single member, where would the body be? As it is, there are many members, yet one body.
1 Corinthians 12:17-20

WHAT YOU'LL NEED:

- craft sticks

- several small, unpainted wooden boxes with lids (available at most craft stores)

- screws

- screwdriver

- ½ inch wooden dowels

- lengths of 1" x ¼ inch wooden boards

- hacksaw

- ruler

The kalimba (kah LEEM bah), also called the *mbira*, is often referred to as the "African thumb piano." The kalimba is made of several thin metal or wooden tongues attached to a box resonator. The resonator may be wood or even a dried gourd. The player plucks the tongues with the thumbs.

BEFORE THE KIDDOS ARRIVE

As you can see by some of the tools, you'll need to do some prep work for this one.

First, you'll need to cut the dowels and the boards to lengths equal to the width of the box. So if the top of each box measures 6 inches across, the dowels and boards need to be cut to those lengths.

Cut the wooden box tops into two equal sections. A 6- by 6-inch top will be cut into two 3- by 6-inch pieces.

Finally, attach the board to the 3- by 6-inch top piece using two screws as shown here. Do not screw the board all the way flush with the lid. Leave a little space.

Granted, this is a lot of prep work, but the final result is really cool.

MAKE A KALIMBA

Give each child a wooden box with a lid, a wooden dowel, and eight craft sticks. The craft sticks often come in assorted colors.

Have the children put the lids on their boxes.

Next, have them slide each of their craft sticks through the space between the lid and the board, with each successive stick pushed in a little more (see photo on pg. 49).

Next, have the children put their dowel between the craft sticks and the lid to hold the sticks in place.

PLUCK THE KALIMBA

Have the children pluck the craft sticks with their thumbs. Invite them to experiment with the lengths of the craft sticks and how that affects the sound.

Ask: "What if all of the sticks were pushed in to the same length?"

THE KAZOOKA

*They shall beat their sword into plowshares,
and their spears into pruning hooks;
nation shall not lift up sword against nation,
neither shall they learn war any more.*
Isaiah 2:4b

The kazooka is an instrument I made up one day. It sounds like a kazoo, but it looks like a bazooka. Kazooka—get it?

BEFORE THE KIDDOS ARRIVE

Cut the 1 ½-inch pipes into 30-inch lengths. You can get pipe in 60-inch lengths, which means cutting these in half.

Cut the 1-inch pipes into 4-inch lengths. Cut the ½-inch pipes into 10-inch lengths.

MAKE A KAZOOKA

Give each child two 30-inch lengths of 1 ½-inch pipe, one 4-inch length of 1-inch pipe, one 10-inch length of ½-inch pipe, a tee, and an elbow.

Then give each child 4 sheets of aluminum foil (about 3 by 3 inches each).

Have the children assemble the kazookas.

Have the children place foil sheets on either side of the T-junction, leaving enough space for air to pass over the sheet.

Connect the two 30-inch pipes to the T-junction, one on either side. Connecting the pipes will hold the foil sheets in place.

Have the children peel away any excess foil.

At the bottom of the T-junction, attach the 4-inch piece, the elbow, and the 10-inch piece.

Note: The kazooka shown uses PVC pipes that are larger than those recommended here.

WHAT YOU'LL NEED:

- PVC pipes 1 ½ inches wide
- PVC pipes 1 inch wide
- PVC pipes ½ inch wide
- 1 ½ inch elbows (90 degrees)
- 1 ½ - 1 inch tee-shaped fitting
- aluminum foil
- hacksaw

PLAY THE KAZOOKA

The 10-inch piece of pipe is the mouthpiece.

Have each child hold the kazooka with the large pipe resting on the shoulder and the mouthpiece right in front of the mouth.

Have the children hum into the mouthpieces of their kazookas. The humming causes the aluminum foil inside to vibrate.

Invite the children to experiment with all the sounds, high and low, loud and soft, they can make with their kazookas.

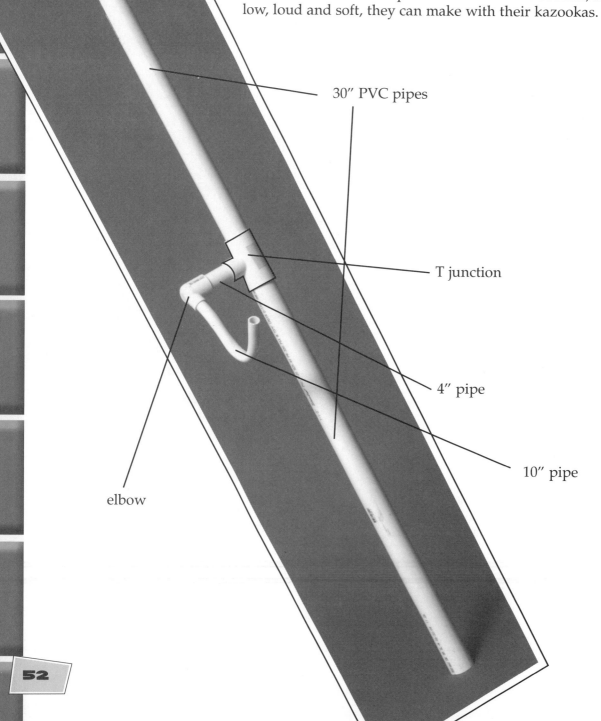

30" PVC pipes

T junction

4" pipe

10" pipe

elbow

DRUMS, DRUMS, AND MORE DRUMS

Raise a song, sound the tambourine.
Psalm 81:2a

A drum is a membranophone. In other words, it is a skin (either hide or plastic) stretched over a frame or vessel.

The first time I ever made drums in church school, one of the parents came up after class and said, "The drums are cool, but there aren't any drums in the Bible." My first thoughts were, "That can't be! Of course there are drums in the Bible! Virtually every culture on the planet has some form of drum! Are you trying to tell me that the only peoples who didn't have drums were those referred to in the Bible?"

Then I went home and looked it up in my New Revised Standard Version Bible. First, I searched all the familiar passages that contain musical instruments—Psalm 150; Genesis 4:21; and 2 Samuel 6:5. Although there is no mention of drumsets, I found plenty of Scriptures containing tambourines, cymbals, and sistrums. The drumset is kind of like a modern version of ancient Hebrew and Egyptian percussive instruments.

And then I turned to the one place that has always held answers to my most obscure questions . . . the Internet. Bingo!

As it turns out, the word *tambourine* found in so many of the passages comes from the Hebrew word *tof*, which is a frame drum with no jingles. In fact, there are several possible translations for *tof*, including "drum," "frame drum," "tambourine," and "timbrel." While scholars do not agree on the exact translation for every instance of the word *tof*, many feel that the translation should be based on the context. What is a "tambourine" in one setting may be a "frame drum" in another. Makes sense, right? Besides, drums are fun to make and even more fun to play. So let's make some drums.

There are many different ways to make all kinds of drums. The following are just a few examples.

A SMALL HAND DRUM

WHAT YOU'LL NEED:

- plastic souvenir cups

- medium-size latex balloons

- scissors

- colored masking tape

- colored electrical tape

- hacksaw or utility knife

- optional: plastic bag

BEFORE THE KIDDOS ARRIVE

Cut off the bottoms of each of the plastic cups using a hacksaw or utility knife. Make sure the plastic cups are made of hard, sturdy plastic. Use a piece of electrical tape to seal the cut end of each cup.

Be aware of any children with latex allergies, and be prepared to offer substitutes. In this case, a piece of plastic cut from a garbage bag or plastic sealable bag will work.

MAKE A SMALL HAND DRUM

Give each child a plastic cup, a roll of colored masking tape, and a pair of scissors. Have the children use the masking tape to cover the outside of their cups.

Next, give each child a roll of colored electrical tape. Have the children put a ring of electrical tape around the top edge and bottom edge of their cups.

Give each child a balloon. Instruct the children to inflate and deflate their balloons a few times to make the material more pliable.

Next, have them cut drum heads from their balloons. Have them each stretch their drum head over the top opening of their cup, pulling the drum head over the sides of the cup until the tension of the drum head holds it in place. There is no need to tape the drum head to the cup.

Once the balloon drum head is on the cup, some of the drums may look a little warped. Help the children even the tension of their drums by pulling on all sides of the cup until the top returns to its circular shape.

For younger children, divide them into pairs. Have one child hold the cup while the other stretches the balloon over the top. Then have the pairs switch roles.

If a piece of plastic bag is used instead of latex, have the children tape the plastic in place. Then have the children cut away any excess plastic.

PLAY THE HAND DRUM

Invite the children to lightly tap their small hand drums using their hands and fingers. It may be necessary to help the children tighten their drum heads a little.

BINGO, BANGO, BONGOS

Bongos are an attached pair of small drums of Afro-Cuban origin. The bongos are typically held between the knees and played with the hands and fingers.

BEFORE THE KIDDOS ARRIVE

Cut off the bottoms of each plastic cup and seal the edges with electrical tape. Then cut two holes, one above the other, down the side of each cup, as shown in the diagram. To save time, cut the cardboard into 6- by 1-inch strips. The materials and design of the bongos are very similar to those of the small hand drum.

MAKE BONGOS

The process for making bongos is quite similar to that of making small hand drums.

Give each child two plastic cups (of different sizes), a roll of colored masking tape, and a pair of scissors. Have the children use the tape to decorate the outsides of each cup. It's okay if the holes get covered with tape.

Next, give each child a roll of colored electrical tape. Have the children put a ring of electrical tape around the bottom edge and top edge of each cup.

Give each child a cardboard strip and a piece of clear tape.

Have the children fold the strips into small trapezoids as shown in the diagram. Have the children secure the shape using the tape.

Give each child four metal paper fasteners. Instruct the children to push the paper fasteners from the inside of each cup out through the holes.

Then have the children push the paper fasteners through the cardboard trapezoid and attach as shown in the diagram.

WHAT YOU'LL NEED:

- plastic souvenir cups (two different sizes)
- medium-size latex balloons
- colored masking tape
- colored electrical tape
- scissors
- metal paper fasteners (four per set of bongos)
- large pieces of corrugated cardboard
- clear packing tape
- hacksaw
- optional: plastic bags

Give each child two balloons. Have them inflate and deflate the balloons a few times to make the material more pliable.

Have the children cut the balloons to form drum heads.

Then have the children stretch the balloons over each cup. You may choose to divide the children into pairs so they may help each other.

Help the children even out the tension of each balloon until the drum heads are uniformly round.

Note: As with the small hand drum, pieces cut from plastic bags may be used in place of latex balloons. Pull the plastic tightly over the top of each cup and secure with tape. Then cut away any excess tape.

PLAY THE BONGOS

Have the children hold the bongos between their knees and lightly tap the drum heads with their hands and fingers. Invite the children to listen for the difference between the two drums in their set of bongos. The larger drum should have a lower sound, and the smaller drum should have a higher sound. If for some children this proves not to be the case, help them tighten the drum head on the smaller drum. A loose drum head will make the sound lower, no matter what size the drum itself.

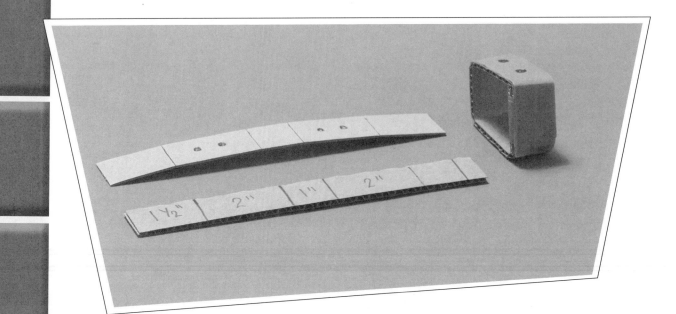

THE DOUMBEK

The doumbek (DOOM bek), also called the *darabuka*, is a goblet-shaped drum of the Middle East. The body of the doumbek may be made of clay, wood, or metal. The player holds the doumbek horizontally in the lap and plays with the palms and fingers.

BEFORE THE KIDDOS ARRIVE

The doumbek takes a little more prep work than some of the other instruments. But the end result is well worth it.

Cut off the bottoms of each plastic cup and seal the edges with electrical tape.

Cut a large hole in the bottom of each plastic bowl, leaving the bowl-like shape intact. Seal off the cut edges of the bowls with electrical tape as well.

MAKE A DOUMBEK

Give each child a plastic cup, a plastic bowl, a roll of colored masking tape, and a pair of scissors. Push the bottom of the cup into the bowl slightly, about ½" to 1". Secure the bottom of the bowl to the bottom of the cup with tape, as shown here. This will give the doumbek its characteristic goblet shape.

Next, allow the children to decorate the outside of each cup and bowl using the tape.

Give each child a roll of colored electrical tape. Have the children put a ring of electrical tape around each edge, as well as a ring around the point where the cup and bowl come together. This ring, while decorative, is there to reinforce the connection between the cup and bowl.

Give each child a medium-large balloon. (Since the mouth of most bowls is larger than the average cup, a larger balloon is needed for the drum head.) Have the children inflate and deflate the balloons several times, then cut the balloons to form a drumhead.

57

Have the children stretch the balloon over the opening of the bowl.

Help each child even the tension of the balloons until each drum head is uniformly round.

You may choose to divide the children into pairs for this step.

It is not necessary to tape the balloons to the bowl. The tension of the balloon, combined with the electrical tape will be enough. If, however, pieces cut from plastic bags are used as a substitute for latex balloons, the children will need to secure the plastic with tape and cut away the excess.

PLAY THE DOUMBEK

Have the children hold their doumbeks horizontally across the thigh. Invite the children to play the doumbek by tapping lightly with the palms and fingers. It may be necessary to help some children tighten their drum heads a little.

THE TAMBOURINE

Then the prophet Miriam, Aaron's sister, took a tambourine in her hand; and all the women went out after her with tambourines and with dancing.
Exodus 15:20

The tambourine, also called the timbrel, originated in the Middle East. A frame drum with jingles set in it, the tambourine may have a head or not.

BEFORE THE KIDDOS ARRIVE
Cut posterboard into strips the full length of the posterboard and four inches wide.

MAKE A TAMBOURINE
Give each child a strip of posterboard, a pair of scissors, and a few pieces of clear tape. Have the children mold their strips into circular frames, overlapping to form a doubly thick frame.

Have the children secure the frames in place using the tape.

Have the children cut four rectangular holes into the frame as shown in the photo. Use a paper punch to start the holes.

Give each child four plastic coffee stirrers. Have the children cut the coffee stirrers to the width of the frame.

Then give each child an assortment of washers. Have the children place a few washers on each coffee stirrer and attach the coffee stirrers to the frames using the clear tape.

If time allows, have the children punch two more holes into their frames. Give each child a ribbon to thread through the holes as decoration for the tambourine.

WHAT YOU'LL NEED:

- yardstick
- posterboard
- scissors
- clear tape
- paper punch
- plastic coffee stirrers
- metal washers
- ribbon

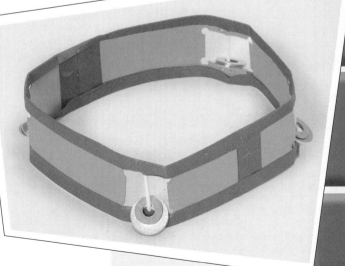

PLAY THE TAMBOURINE

Invite the children to explore the many ways they can play their tambourines.

They can hold the instrument with one hand and tap the frame with the other.

They can shake the tambourine back and forth. They can lightly tap the individual jingles.

They can perform a combination of these methods.

STRINGED INSTRUMENTS

Awake my soul! Awake, O harp and lyre! I will awake the dawn.
Psalm 57:8

There are numerous references in the Bible to stringed instruments such as the harp, lyre, psaltery, and viol. In fact, there are over a dozen references just in the Book of Psalms. What book on making instruments, especially a book for use in church schools, would be complete without stringed instruments?

But here's the thing—stringed instruments are very tricky.

First, there is the whole tuning issue. Most string instruments, from harps to guitars, require the strings to be tuned to different (not to mention accurate) pitches. Building instruments that require that kind of precision is pretty tough to do in one hour!

Second, there is the volume issue. Plucking a string just doesn't produce as much sound as banging a drum. Almost all string instruments need some kind of resonator to project the sound of the strings. There are many ways to make resonators, but these tend to be either very time consuming or visually distracting once made.

WHAT YOU'LL NEED:

- harp pattern (pg. 94)
- cardboard
- scissors
- phillip's head screwdriver or metal compass
- clear packing tape
- crayons or markers
- rubber bands

THE HARP

The harp is an ancient instrument. The oldest harp was found at Ur, and is believed to date back to 2600 B.C. Harps can have any number of strings.

BEFORE THE KIDDOS ARRIVE

Use the harp pattern (pg. 94) to trace and cut out the harp frame from the cardboard (two frames per harp). Older children may be able to do this step for themselves.

Punch holes where indicated in the pattern using a Phillip's head screwdriver (or a metal compass).

MAKE A HARP

Give each child two cardboard harp frames. Next, give each child a few assorted crayons or markers and allow the children to decorate the harp frames. Then, with the clear packing tape, have the children tape the two frames together into one strong one. Make sure the children keep the holes lined up.

Then give each child five rubber bands and a pair of scissors.

Have the children cut the rubber bands into cords. Then have the children attach the rubber cords to the harp frame by threading and tying each end through one of the holes.

The end result will be a five-string harp.

PLAY THE HARP

Have the children hold their harps vertically and pluck the individual cords. Invite them to listen to the difference in sound of each of the cords.

Normally, the longer strings on a harp will sound lower than the small ones. With this particular harp, the longer cords will produce higher sounds. Why?

The reason is that while the cords are longer, they are also pulled tighter because they have to be pulled over a longer distance. This makes the cord thinner, and, in one respect, smaller.

Here are a few ways to counter this:
1. Cut each rubber band into a cord of a different length, so that the shorter lengths will have to be pulled tighter.
2. Tie the longest cord as loose as possible, and increase the tightness as the cords get smaller.
3. Use rubber bands in a variety of sizes, the larger rubber bands for the longer cords.

This harp will also be quite soft, since it does not have a resonator. This might be a blessing in disguise.

THE BERIMBAU

The berimbau (buh REEM bau) is a musical bow, which while of African origin, was made popular as an accompaniment instrument to the capoeira dances of Brazil. Capoeira is a martial art dance developed over four hundred years ago by African slaves in Brazil. One theory suggests that these dances were performed to train slaves to use martial arts as a way to escape captivity. In this theory, the berimbau player is important. The player would accompany the training with specific rhythms while serving as a lookout for the slave masters. If a master approached, the player would slightly alter the rhythm, signaling for the dancers to change their movements to something less conspicuous. In this way, the berimbau rhythms would be similar to many African-American songs and spirituals, which were believed to contain hidden messages.

BEFORE THE KIDDOS ARRIVE

Wash and dry all of the cans.

Use the hammer and nail to punch two holes in the bottom of each can.

Use a saw to cut notches into either end of a yardstick or wooden dowel.

MAKE A BERIMBAU

Give each child a yardstick (or dowel) and a guitar string.

Have the children tie one end of the guitar string around one end of the yardstick.

Next, have the children slightly bend the yardsticks until they have a bow-like bend.

Have the children tie the loose end of the guitar string to the other end of the yardstick. The string should be tight and the yardstick slightly bent. You may wish to divide the children into pairs for this step. They can help each other by having one bend the yardstick while the other ties the string in place. Then the children can switch roles.

WHAT YOU'LL NEED:

- coffee can
- hammer
- nails
- saw
- yardsticks
- guitar string
- sturdy fishing line
- unsharpened pencils

63

Next, give each child a can and a twelve-inch length of sturdy fishing line. Instruct the children to place the bottom of their cans to the bow. Have the children tie the cans in place using the fishing line. The fishing line should wrap around not only the bow, but also the yardstick and the guitar string as well. The can will serve as the resonator.

PLAY THE BERIMBAU

Give each child an unsharpened pencil.

Have each child hold the stick part of his or her berimbau with one hand and tap the string with the pencil.

Invite the children to explore the pitch possibilities by bending the bow slightly as they play. Then have the children release the tension as they tap the string.

In the spirit of the berimbau player of old:

As a group, create a few rhythms that can serve as code for certain phrases.

For example, a rhythm of long—short—short could mean "Good morning."

Short—short—short—short—short—short—long could mean "Jesus loves me, this I know."

Once the group has created a few code rhythms, choose a child to play one of these rhythms on his or her berimbau. The others must guess the phrase that goes with that rhythm.

Allow each child a chance to play a code rhythm.

THE DOLLAR STORE DJEMBE

*Create in me a clean heart, O God,
and put a new and right spirit within me.*
Psalm 51:10

The djembe (JEM beh) is a large, goblet-shaped drum of West African origin. In recent years the djembe has become very popular, finding its way into everything from community drum circles to mainstream pop music.

BEFORE THE KIDDOS ARRIVE

Cut off the bottoms of each plastic trash can with a hacksaw, and seal the edges with packing tape. With a utility knife, cut a large hole out of the bottom of each bowl, leaving the bowl-like shape intact. Seal the cut edge of each bowl with the packing tape.

MAKE A DOLLAR STORE DJEMBE

Give each child a plastic trash can, a plastic bowl, a roll of colored packing tape, and a pair of scissors. Have the children secure the bottom of each bowl to the bottom of a trash can using a few pieces of tape. This will give the djembe its goblet-like shape.

Next, have the children place the plastic lids onto the bowls and secure in place with tape from inside the bowls.

Allow the children to decorate their djembes using the colored packing tape.

Note: The design for the djembe is similar to that of the smaller doumbek.

WHAT YOU'LL NEED:

- plastic trash cans
- hacksaw
- plastic bowls with lids
- utility knife
- colored packing tape
- scissors

PLAY THE DJEMBE

Have the children hold their djembes between their knees, perpendicular to the floor. Invite the children to use their palms and fingers to play the drum heads. Have the children explore the different sound possibilities depending on where the drum head is struck.

EFFECTIVE SOUND EFFECTS

Make a joyful noise to the LORD, all the earth.
Psalm 100:1

Here are some simple noisemakers and sound effects instruments you can make to help bring a Bible story to life.

COMB CRICKET

Rub your thumb along the teeth of a plastic comb to create a singing cricket sound. Or you can rub the teeth against the edge of a desk.

CUP HOOVES

Use two overturned plastic cups on a hard, flat surface to simulate the sound of a horse's hooves.

RAIN

Roll a sheet of wax paper into a cone. Fold the tip of the cone. Use a salt shaker to sprinkle salt into the cone, creating a light rain sound.

BOING!

Hold a plastic ruler onto a flat surface with one hand so that a small part of the ruler is hanging off the side. Pluck the ruler with your free hand.

Try sliding the ruler out as you pluck to make the pitch get lower. Slide the ruler in as you pluck to make the pitch get higher.

WHAT YOU'LL NEED:

- plastic comb
- plastic cups
- wax paper
- salt shaker
- plastic ruler
- cardboard tube
- plastic straw
- pencil

QUACK!

Cut a plastic drinking straw about three inches long. Flatten one end slightly and cut as shown in the photo. This creates two points. Place the two plastic points between your lips. Apply gentle pressure as you blow to create a duck call.

KAZOO

Use the pencil to punch a hole into the center of the tube.

Place the wax paper sheet over one end of the tube and secure the sheet in place with the rubber band. Hum into the open end of the tube to create a buzzing sound.

These and other sound effects instruments can be used to tell a story. Or you can simply use them as noisemakers for the following musical activity.

ESTHER—A MUSICAL SOUND EFFECTS STORY

During the Jewish festival Purim, the story of Esther is read. It is tradition to use graggers to make noise each time Haman's name is said, so that no one will hear the name of Haman.

Let's take this one step further.

Give each child a copy of the following story, as well as a noisemaker.

Assign each noisemaker to the name of one of the people in the story.

When someone's name comes up in the story, have the child or children play the noisemaker that corresponds to that name.

Here are possible noisemakers for each person in the story.

Xerxes – kazoo
Esther – Boing! ruler
Haman – Quack! straw

Vashti – cricket comb
Mordecai – cup hooves

Xerxes, the king of Persia, held a big feast that lasted several days. **Xerxes** sent for his wife, **Vashti**, so that everyone could see her. But **Vashti** refused to come, and that made **Xerxes** very mad. He declared that **Vashti** would not be queen anymore, and that he would choose a new wife from the many beautiful women.

One of these women was **Esther**; she was an orphan who had been adopted by **Mordecai**, a Jewish man who worked in the palace. King **Xerxes** fell in love with **Esther** and married her, not knowing she was Jewish.

Haman, the king's second in command, hated **Mordecai**, and wanted to get rid of all the Jewish people. **Mordecai** discovered **Haman's** plot and asked **Esther** to tell **Xerxes** about it.

Esther was very nervous. She would be in big trouble if she went to **Xerxes** without being invited. But she found the courage to invite King **Xerxes** to a banquet the next day.

That same night, **Xerxes** remembered that **Mordecai** had once saved his life. He wanted to reward **Mordecai** and asked **Haman** for advice. **Haman** thought King **Xerxes** wished to reward him, so he advised that the reward should be to ride in a procession wearing royal clothes. King **Xerxes** liked the idea. "All right!" he said, "Prepare all this for **Mordecai**!"

Haman was very upset. He wanted to get rid of **Mordecai**, not honor him. That evening at the banquet, **Esther** revealed to King **Xerxes** that she was Jewish, and that **Haman** was planning to get rid of her people.

King **Xerxes** punished **Haman** and rewarded **Mordecai** with a royal procession. King **Xerxes** then gave **Haman's** job to **Mordecai**. It was a great day for the Jewish people, thanks to the bravery of **Esther**!

ONE-STRING GUITAR

Praise him with strings and pipe!
Psalm 150:4b

WHAT YOU'LL NEED:

- aluminum cans
- hammer
- nail
- wooden bead
- ball end guitar string
- unsharpened pencil
- optional: quilting thread

The one-string guitar is a miniature version of a washtub bass.

BEFORE THE KIDDOS ARRIVE

Wash and dry the cans. Use the hammer and nail to punch a hole in the bottom of each can.

MAKE A ONE-STRING GUITAR

Give each child a can, a wooden bead, and a ball end guitar string.

Thread a wooden bead onto the guitar string. Pull until the bead fits snugly against the inside bottom of the can. Thread the guitar string through the hole in the can with the ball end on the outside of the bead.

Next, give each child an unsharpened pencil. Have the children wind the loose end of the guitar string around the pencil.

STRUM THE ONE-STRING GUITAR

Invite the children to sit in chairs, holding the pencil in one hand. Instruct the children to place both feet on the overturned can.

Have the children pluck the string with one hand as they tighten and loosen it by pulling the pencil.

Easy option: Use strong quilting thread instead of a guitar string.

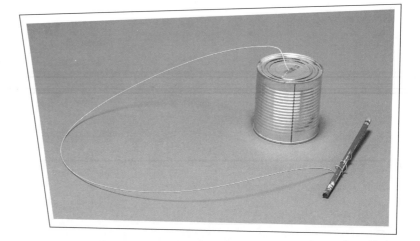

SOME SIMPLE GIFTS

The unfolding of your words gives light;
it imparts understanding to the simple.
Psalm 119:130

Two of the most important instruments in any rhythm section are the bass drum and the rhythm sticks (or claves). The bass drum serves part of the timekeeping function, holding the steady beat for the rest of the group.

The rhythm sticks often play offbeat rhythms that can be heard quite well, because of the cutting sound of the wood. Here are a few simple ways to add bass drum and claves to your collection of instruments. No prep work or construction is required—just an active imagination.

BASS DRUMS

An empty, five-gallon plastic water bottle makes a great bass drum. So does a large cardboard box, or an overturned, large, plastic trash can.

The bass drum can be played with the hands or with a mallet.

You can make a mallet by drilling a hole into a rubber ball and fitting it snugly on a twelve-inch wooden dowel.

CLAVES/RHYTHM STICKS

A pair of unsharpened pencils makes a fine set of rhythm sticks. A pair of short, thick, wooden dowels works well as a set of claves.

WHAT YOU'LL NEED:

- five-gallon plastic water bottle, cardboard box, or large plastic trash can

- optional: mallet or rubber ball and 12-inch wooden dowel

WHAT YOU'LL NEED:

- unsharpened pencils or short, thick wooden dowels

MAKING MUSIC IN THE CLASSROOM

Make a joyful noise to the Lord, all the earth.
Worship the Lord with gladness;
come into his presence with singing.
Psalm 100:1-2

So far we've focused our attention on making musical instruments. Almost every instrument can be made with time to spare for actually making music.

There are so many ways to incorporate musical instruments into lessons and activities. Here are just a few:

1. Play a rhythmic passing game.
2. Play a percussion jam.
3. Create a tone poem.
4. Create incidental music for the dramatic reading of a Bible story.
5. Create a sound track for a video clip.
6. Play a rhythmic call-and-response game.
7. Accompany a Bible song with instruments.
8. Use instruments to reinforce a speech percussion piece.
9. Create a musical sound effects story, substituting people's names with sounds.

RHYTHMIC PASSING GAMES

WHAT YOU'LL NEED

• beanbags

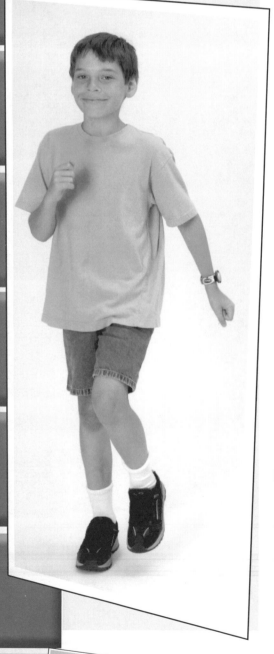

PASS THE STEADY BEAT

Invite the children to sit with you in a circle on the floor. Have the children tap their thighs to the beat as they count a steady four-pattern with you (1-2-3-4-1-2-3-4, and so forth).

Next, while the children continue to count, pass a small beanbag around the circle, making sure that each child passes the ball on the beat.

After the beanbag has made it around the circle a few times, pass around a second beanbag, then a third. See how many beanbags you and the children can keep going around to the steady beat. Try the activity again, this time having the children think, rather than speak, the four-pattern.

Give each child a musical instrument. Now, instead of passing a beanbag around the circle, pass the steady beat. Start by inviting the children to count the four-pattern aloud. Play your instrument on beat one and have the child to your right play on beat two, and so on.

After the beat has made it around the circle a few times, pass it around again, adding another beat. See if you and the children can keep two beats going around the circle. Try to pass the beats around again, this time having the children think, rather than speak, the four-pattern.

This game is fun by itself, but it can also serve as a great warmup for other rhythm activities. The passing game reinforces the steady beat while illustrating that every player does not have to play on every beat in order to keep the music going. This game also helps the group come together as a whole, which is important socially as well as for good ensemble playing.

PATTERN PASS

Invite the children to sit with you in a circle on the floor. Hold a small beanbag and say: "I am going to gently toss this beanbag to someone. Whoever I toss it to must toss it to someone else, and so on until each person in the circle has caught the beanbag. The last one holding the beanbag must toss it to me. Also, remember who tossed the beanbag to you, as well as the person to whom you tossed the beanbag."

Choose a child and make eye contact. Then hold up the beanbag and toss it gently to that child.

That child must choose another, make eye contact, and gently toss the beanbag to that child.

Have the children do this until each child has caught the beanbag and it comes back to you.

Then toss it back to the child whom you tossed it to before.

Once the children are comfortable tossing the beanbag from person to person, add another beanbag, and another. See if you and the children can keep three beanbags going at one time.

The eye contact is an important part of this activity. So much of the communication that goes on between musicians is nonverbal. Make sure the children never toss the beanbag to someone until they have made eye contact. Also, remind the children that once they have tossed the beanbag, they should look to the person who tosses it to them. This reinforces the important musical skill of thinking about what comes next.

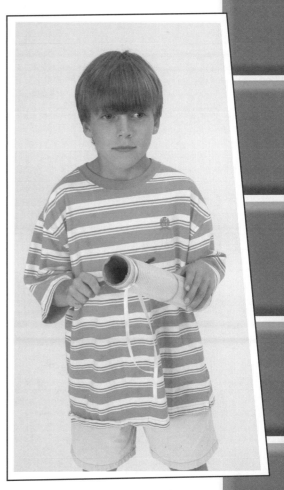

Once you and the children have established the passing pattern using beanbags, give each child a different musical instrument.

Now, instead of passing a beanbag around the pattern, pass a sound.

Start by making eye contact with the same child you did before, and play one sound on your instrument. You have passed the sound to that child.

Have that child do the same until the sound has been passed all the way around the pattern and back to you.

Here is a fun variation on this game that helps develop critical listening skills.

Pass the sound around the pattern, instructing the children to listen closely to the sound that comes right before the one they play.

Next, have the children close their eyes. Pass the sound around the pattern, this time without any visual cues. The children must use their ears to recognize when the sound is being passed to them.

PERCUSSION JAMS

One of the most exciting musical experiences is the percussion jam. The sound of all those drums, rattles, claves, bells, and other percussion instruments put together can be electrifying!

Percussion jams are great for building community, exploring the importance of diversity, illustrating the value of cooperation, and reinforcing important biblical concepts.

There are several composed percussion jams provided in this resource (pages 99-108). Each jam contains multiple rhythms to be played together. Each rhythm is set to a word or short phrase, such as a parable or proverb, which helps reinforce a biblical concept. The following is a process that works well for teaching any of these percussion jams.

Have the children sit with you in a circle on the floor.

Have the children listen as you speak one of the phrases in rhythm. Then have the children echo the phrase. Do this for all the phrases and rhythms in the jam.

Next, have the children speak each phrase in rhythm while tapping or clapping the rhythm. Then have the children clap or tap each rhythm while thinking, rather than speaking, the phrase.

Give each child an instrument. Have the children play each rhythm on their instruments. Divide the children into as many groups as there are different rhythms in the percussion jam. Assign one rhythm to each of the groups. Lead each group as they play their rhythm.

Have the other groups listen and imagine how their particular rhythm will fit with the one being played.

Once each group can play their rhythm confidently, start putting rhythms together. Have one group play their rhythm and repeat it over and over. Once that group is playing steadily, bring in another group to play their rhythm with the first rhythm. It may take a few attempts to get the two groups to play their different rhythms together.

Once the two groups are playing together, add a third group, and so on.

When children are first learning how to play a percussion jam, it may work best to have only two groups play at one time.

When putting a jam together, the rhythm train is bound to get derailed from time to time. Here are some ideas for how to get that train back on track.

1. Groups have a natural tendency to speed up. Remind the children to keep the beat steady.

2. If the children have difficulty playing one rhythm while hearing another, go back to speaking the phrase. Those few words can make the abstract concept of rhythm seem amazingly concrete.

3. Make sure to assign appropriate instruments to the different parts. Many of the jams in this resource include instrument suggestions. Those suggestions are based on which instruments work best for particular rhythms. For example, assigning a very busy rhythm to a bass drum can make the rhythm sound blurry.

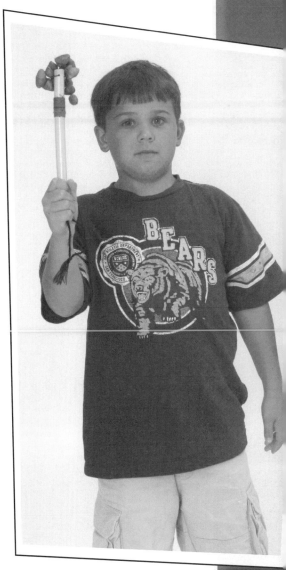

4. Each percussion jam contains simple as well as more complex rhythms. Layer the jam by starting with the simple rhythms. In fact, the more complex rhythms could be played by soloists, rather than small groups.

5. Rotate instruments and rhythms. One child may be a whiz at the complex rhythms, but have difficulty with the steady beat. Another child may embrace the regularity of that steady beat. One child may thrive on the shekere, while another excels at hand drumming. Allow the children the chance to explore many instruments and rhythms. Help them build on their strengths.

By the way, you don't need any instruments to enjoy the percussion jams. Body percussion can make an excellent substitute for instruments. You can also perform the percussion jams as speech percussion. The rhythmic speech of the phrases helps internalize the rhythms as well as the messages in the phrases spoken.

After jamming for a while, you can play this fun game as a review: Choose a child to play one of the rhythms from the jam. The others must guess the word or phrase that corresponds to that rhythm. Allow each child a chance to play a rhythm.

CREATE A TONE POEM

A tone poem is a musical form in which the instruments portray a story, scene, or mood. You can easily turn a favorite Bible story or psalm into a tone poem.

Have the children sit with you in a circle on the floor. Read a story or psalm from the Bible. Then place several instruments in the center of the circle. Read the story again, this time inviting the children to think of people, things, actions, or moods that can be represented by the musical instruments.

Once you have read the story, have the children list all the people, things, actions, and moods that could be represented by a musical instrument. Write this list down on a chalkboard or posterboard in the chronological order of the story.

Allow the children a few minutes to explore the different instruments and decide which instruments can represent certain parts of the story. Write each instrument next to the word or phrase it is to depict. Assign a different musical instrument to each child. Read the story again, this time having each child play his or her instrument when the corresponding word or phrase comes up.

The final step in creating the tone poem is to have the children play the instruments without having the story spoken. Let the instruments do the talking.

With younger children, use icons (simple pictures) to represent the words as well as the instruments to be used.

After the children have performed the tone poem, they can play this fun game as a review: Have the children close their eyes. Say: "I will quietly tap one of you on the shoulder. Whoever I tap must play his or her instrument." Once the child has played the instrument, have the others open their eyes. They must first guess who played the instrument. Then they must recall which part of the story that instrument depicted. Allow each child a chance to play his or her instrument.

On the following page is a Bible story with suggested instrumentation for a tone poem.

THE BOY'S LUNCH

THE STORY IN WORDS

One day Jesus crossed
the Sea of Galilee.

When he reached the other side,
a huge crowd gathered
to watch him cure the sick.

As the sun began to set,
the disciples said, "It is
getting late, and the people
have nothing to eat."

"Then give them something
to eat," Jesus replied. One
of the disciples said to him,
"There is a boy here who has
five barley loaves and two fish.
But what are they among
so many people?"

Jesus said, "Make the people
sit down." So the people,
about five thousand in all,
went to a grassy place
and sat down.

Then Jesus took the loaves, and
when he had given thanks, he
broke the loaves and gave them
to those who were seated. Then
Jesus did the same with the fish,
as much as the people wanted.

When the people were full,
Jesus told his disciples to gather
all the leftover pieces. The
disciples gathered up enough
pieces to fill twelve baskets.

Play the tone poem again, allowing
the children to try different instruments.

THE STORY IN SOUNDS

Play ocean drum.

Play small hand drums.

Play descending notes on
the panpipes.

Scrape guiro five times,
strike claves two times.

Play small hand drums.

Start playing claves softly,
then gradually add all the
other instruments. Get
louder gradually.
Stop all playing.

Shake rattle
twelve times

SOME HELPFUL HINTS

Here is a very condensed
version of Jonah's story.
Try turning it into a tone
poem with the children
using only body
percussion and
mouth/vocal sounds.

JONAH'S STORY

God commanded.
Jonah fled.
Ship boarded.
Storm approached.
Ship rocked.
Jonah confessed.
Men tossed.
Sea calmed.
Fish gulped.
Jonah thought.
Fish spit.
Jonah obeyed.
Nineveh reached.
People warned.
Ninevites changed.
God forgave.
Jonah perplexed.

INCIDENTAL MUSIC

Incidental music is often used in connection with a play. The music can be before the play, such as an overture. Incidental music can also be used to accompany the action of a play.

Incidental music can accompany the dramatic reading of a Bible story.

Have the children sit with you in a circle on the floor.

Read a Bible story aloud.

Next, place several instruments in the center of the circle.

Read the story again, inviting the children to listen for any people, things, actions, or moods that could be highlighted with the musical instruments.

Make a list of these people, things, actions, or moods on a chalkboard or posterboard.

Invite the children to explore the musical instruments, searching for those that will best highlight those parts of the story.

Write each instrument chosen next to the corresponding part of the story it will highlight.

Assign an instrument to each child and have each child play his or her part when it comes up in the story.

On the following page is a Bible story with suggested instrumentation for incidental music.

JESUS CALMS THE STORM

THE STORY MUSIC	THE INCIDENTAL
One day Jesus and his disciples took a boat to cross the Sea of Galilee.	Play one ocean drum.
Soon a terrible storm arose. The waves crashed and began filling the boat with water.	Play rainstick. Play hand drums. Play all ocean drums.
Meanwhile, Jesus was asleep at the back of the boat, his head on a cushion.	Play tambourines. Continue all other sounds listed above.
The disciples shouted, "Master, don't you care that we are all about to drown?"	Play sistrums. Continue all other sounds listed above.
Jesus woke up and rebuked the wind. Then he called to the sea,"Peace! Be still."	Continue all instruments. After "Peace! Be still," all instruments are silent.
And there was a great calm. Jesus asked the disciples, "Why are you so afraid? Have you no trust in me?"	Remain silent.
The disciples were filled with awe and said to one another, "Who is this Jesus? Even the wind and sea obey him."	Play one ocean drum.

Once the children have performed the incidental music, have them switch instruments and play again.

GOD THE GREAT MUSICIAN

Have the children sit with you in a circle on the floor. Place several clean, recyclable materials, such as plastic soda bottles and cardboard boxes, in the center of the circle. Read the following story, then invite the children to create incidental music for the story using only those materials in the circle.

In the beginning, God the Great Musician decided to sit down and create an orchestra.

God make the trumpeter swan, the goose, and the elephant to sound out bright, brassy fanfares.

God made the horse and the cow to pound percussively with their clip-clop hooves.

Sometimes God wanted to hear gentler sounds, so God made the tree frog, the cardinal, the chickadee, and the owl to chirp, toot, flute, and hoot.

Then God made the virtuoso cricket to fiddle jumping jigs and lyrical lullabies.

And God wanted singing. God made the howler monkey to howl, the grizzly bear to growl, and the whale to sigh sweetly in the sea.

And God heard that it was good.

But something was missing.

God's orchestra needed a conductor. So God created the human to lead the orchestra—not to decide which instruments were necessary, and which ones were not, but to guide God's entire orchestra through holy harmonies.

Under the conductor's care, the orchestra played wonderful symphonies—joyful, mournful, beautiful—every note a celebration of creation and a tribute to God, the greatest musician of all.

Through the years the conductor's baton was passed down from generation to generation.

Some conductors were more in tune with God's music than others. Many of God's instruments grew faint, while others completely disappeared.

Now the baton has been passed to us. We are the conductors of God's miraculous orchestra.

How will the music sound under our care?

COMPOSE A SOUNDTRACK

WHAT YOU'LL NEED

- TV

- DVD or VCR

- video clip

- optional: The Beginner's Bible: The Easter Story

Soundtracks are used in movies and television to heighten the emotion of the events as they unfold.

The children can create a soundtrack to accompany a short video clip.

Have the children watch a short, age-appropriate video clip with the sound turned off. Video clips with plenty of action work best.

Next, allow the children to experiment with different instruments or other objects in the room that could be used to give sound to the video.

Play the video clip again, and have the children accompany the action with their original soundtrack.

Allow the children to try different options as they discover the sounds they prefer for each action.

Challenge the children to watch the video clip carefully in order to synchronize the soundtrack.

For fun, turn the volume back up and have the children listen as they watch the clip. More often than not, the soundtrack the children created is more fresh and original than the one on the video.

Here is a sample video clip with soundtrack suggestions.

Video Soundtrack—The Beginner's Bible: The Easter Story

Cue: 1665
Stop: 1790
Approximate Running Time: two minutes
Scene: Easter morning at the tomb. The stone rolls aside. The Marys enter, and an angel tells them that Jesus has risen and they should go to Galilee and tell the others.

SEQUENCE OF EVENTS
AND POSSIBLE INSTRUMENTATION:

1. The soldiers are playing dice beside the tomb. Roll wooden blocks.

2. The stone begins to move. Hand drum roll.

3. The stone falls. Strike drum loudly.

4. An angel appears. Strum harp.

5. The soldiers run away. Play ascending line on panpipes.

6. The women approach the tomb. Play hand drums slowly.

7. The soldiers run past the women. Play ascending line on panpipes.

8. Mary enters tomb. Play one hand drum slowly.

9. Angel tells Mary the good news. Strum harp.

10. Mary leaves the tomb and startles the others. Play one hand drum slowly.

11. The other women drop items. Strike drums softly.

12. The women run to Galilee. Play hand drums quickly.

CALL AND RESPONSE

There are many instances in the Bible where people respond to a call. God calls Moses and Jonah. Jesus calls the disciples. Call and response is a musical form where a soloist or small group improvises a call and the larger group plays or sings a recurring response.

Have the children sit with you in a circle on the floor. Speak out a call and teach the children to speak the response in rhythm.

Do this for each call, always inviting the children to offer their rhythmic response. Allow each child an opportunity to speak the call.

You can transfer the same call-and-response rhythms to instruments or body percussion.

The following call-and-response is based on the secret symbol of the early Christians, the fish.

GO FISH!

CALL	RESPONSE
Are there any Christians here?	Go fish! Go fish!
Whisper till the coast is clear.	Go fish! Go fish!
First we'll make the secret sign.	Go fish! Go fish!
Then we'll know that all is fine.	Go fish! Go fish!
Swimming creature drawn to scale.	Go fish! Go fish!
That's the sign that tells the tale.	Go fish! Go fish!
Jesus Christ, God's special son.	Go fish! Go fish!
He's our savior. He's the one.	Go fish! Go fish!
I believe, and so do you.	Go fish! Go fish!
Let us follow "you know who."	Go fish! Go fish!

The echo game is similar to a call and response. In the echo game, however, the soloist plays or claps a short rhythm that the others must echo exactly.

This is a great warmup game for sharpening listening skills. Many great musical cultures pass their music on orally and aurally rather than through written notation. Allow each child a chance to lead in the echo game.

PETER AND AENEAS

Peter went to Lydda where he came upon a man.
This man could not stand up at all, but Peter had a plan.

Aeneas, make your bed!

Peter looked right in his eyes and said, "Get on your feet!"
In the name of God's own son, put your toes down on that street!"

Aeneas, make your bed!

"The time for simply sitting there was once but now is gone.
Get on your feet and put away the mat you're sitting on."

Aeneas, make your bed!

And all the folks of Lydda stared at them in great surprise.
They'd never seen a man be healed right before their eyes.

Aeneas, make your bed!

They put away their sinful lives and to the Lord they turned.
The Holy Spirit filled their hearts and with God's love they burned.

Aeneas, make your bed!

Jesus came to show us all how great God's love can be,
and how that love is freely given to folks like you and me.

Aeneas, make your bed!

(Based on Acts 9:32-35)

ACCOMPANY A BIBLE SONG

Children can accompany virtually any song with instruments. Part of the fun is in deciding which instrument, or instruments, work best with a particular song.

A song with a Latin American salsa feel could be enhanced with guiros, claves, and maracas.

A song with a march-like feel could be accompanied by drums and sistrums.

Allow the children to experiment with different instruments as they choose which ones to use.

REINFORCE A SPEECH PERCUSSION PIECE

Each percussion jam in this resource includes texts that reinforce not only the rhythms, but also the Bible concepts.

You may choose to perform these jams using speech percussion rather than instruments.

You may also choose to have the children play the rhythms on instruments as they speak the texts. In this way the spoken word reinforces the rhythms, while the rhythms reinforce the spoken word.

CREATE A MUSICAL SOUND EFFECTS STORY

You can create your own musical sound effects Bible story, like we did for Esther (see page 68), or use the following. Short stories with recurring names work best.

Moses - shofar
Pharaoh - cup hooves
Israelites - tambourine
Red Sea - ocean drum
Angel - harp

Crossing the Red Sea

Pharaoh chased the Israelites.

The **Israelites** looked back and saw Pharaoh and his army approaching.

Moses told the people not to be afraid.

The **angel** of God stood between the Israelites and Pharaoh's army.

The Lord opened the **Red Sea**.

The **Israelites** crossed to the other side in safety.

The Lord closed the **Red Sea** behind them.

A STORY WITH A BEAT

Read the story on the following page.

WHAT YOU'LL NEED:

- hand drums
- bongos
- ocean drum
- doumbek
- cup hooves

Have the children sit with you in a circle on the floor. Read the story on the following page. As you get to a sentence that is in capital letters, teach the children that sentence in rhythm.

After teaching each rhythm, divide the children into five groups. Assign each group a different sentence with a corresponding instrument.

Read the story again. Pause at each capitalized sentence, allowing the assigned group to speak and play the rhythm of that sentence.

Have the children switch groups and read the story with a beat again.

The five parts fit together into a percussion jam. If time allows, have all five parts play together.

DANIEL IN THE LIONS' DEN

Daniel was an Israelite. King Darius was the king of Persia.

DANIEL WAS FRIENDS WITH THE KING.

But some of the king's advisors were jealous of Daniel. They thought of a way to get him in trouble with the king.

SOME MEN WERE JEALOUS.

They asked the king, "Didn't you make a law forbidding people to pray to any god or anyone but you?"

"Yes, I did make that law," answered King Darius. "That law cannot be changed. Anyone who disobeys that law will be thrown into the lions' den."

"Well," said the advisors, "we know for a fact that Daniel prays to his God three times a day."

DANIEL PRAISED GOD THREE TIMES EACH DAY.

King Darius liked Daniel, but the law could not be changed. So Daniel was thrown into the lion's den, and the mouth of the den was sealed with a huge stone.

THEY THREW DANIEL IN THE DEN OF LIONS.

The king went home, but he was too sad to eat or sleep. The next morning he rushed to the lions' den and called out, "Oh, Daniel, has your God, whom you faithfully serve, saved you from the lions?"

"May the king live forever," replied Daniel. "My God sent an angel to shut the lions' mouths, because I have done no wrong."

GOD KEPT THE LIONS FROM HURTING DANIEL.

Then King Darius was very happy and wrote a message for all the people: "All people must worship the God of Daniel. His God is the living God whose kingdom will have no end."

SOME HELPFUL THINGS

BULL-ROARER PATTERN

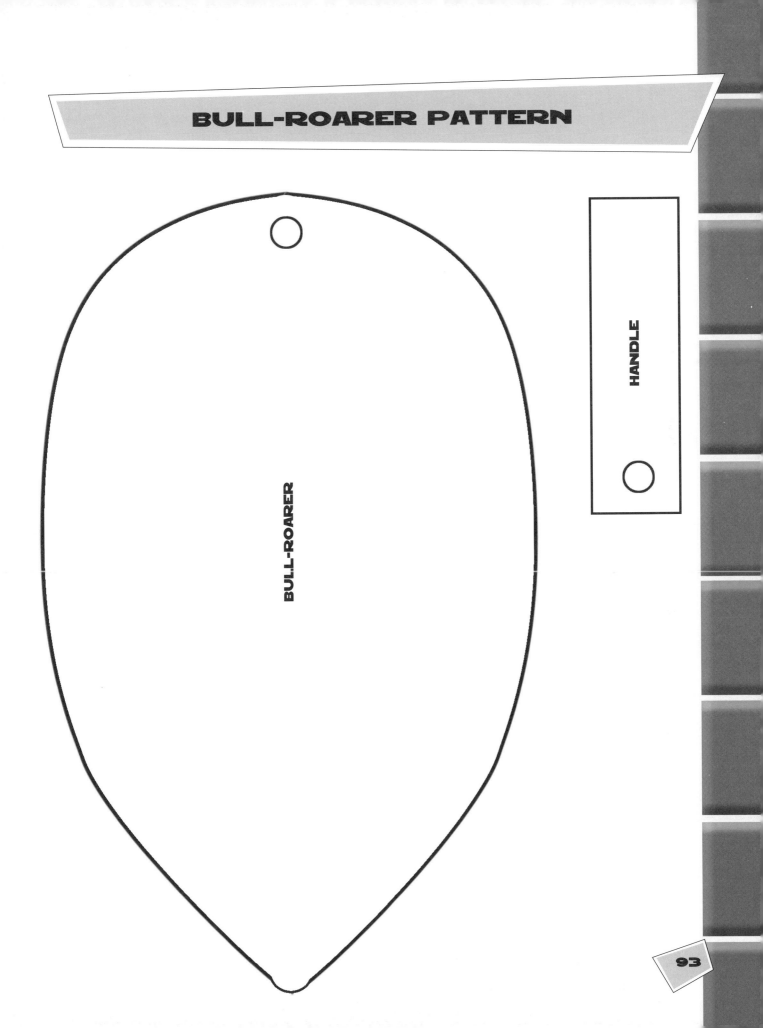

BULL-ROARER

HANDLE

HARP PATTERN

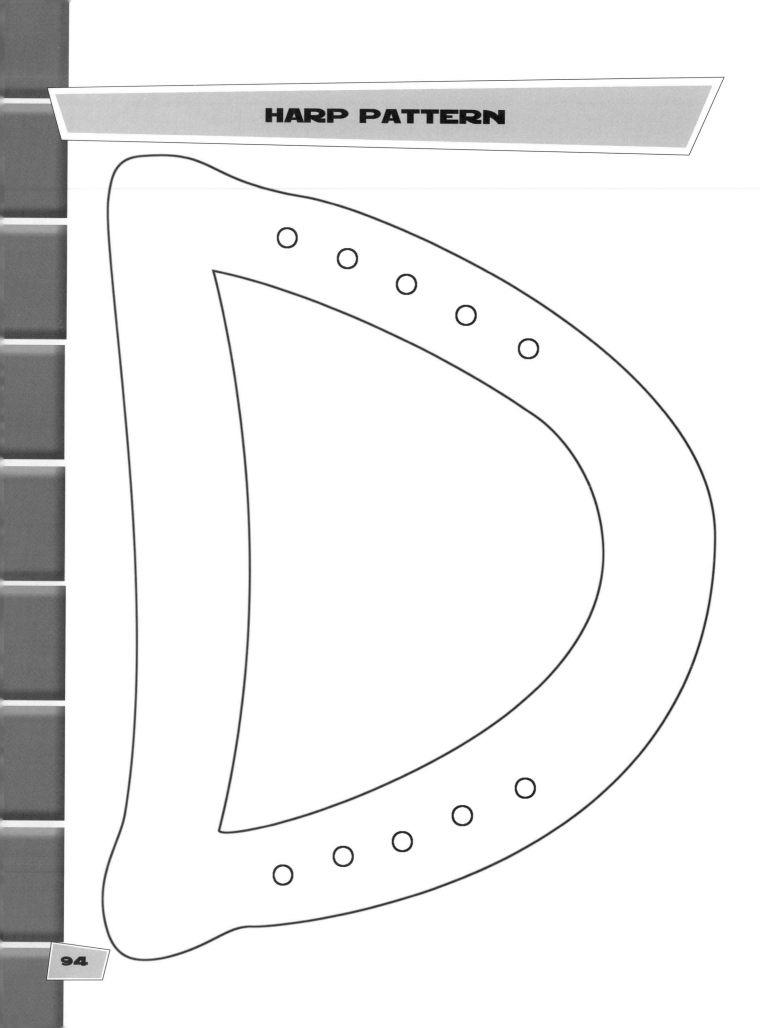

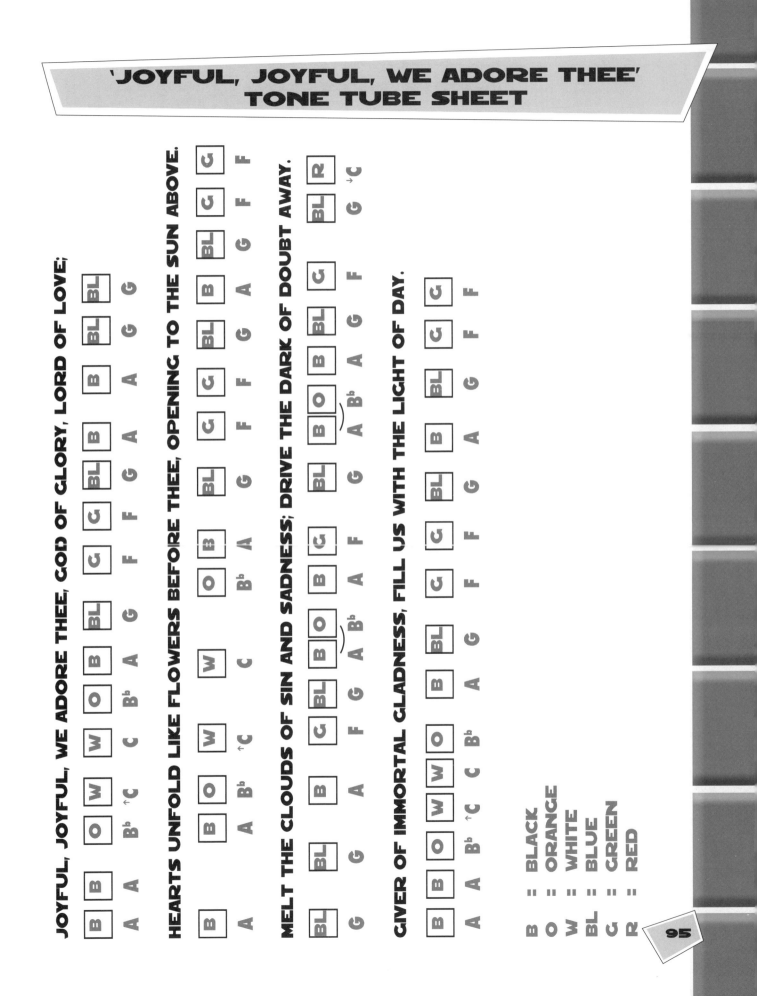

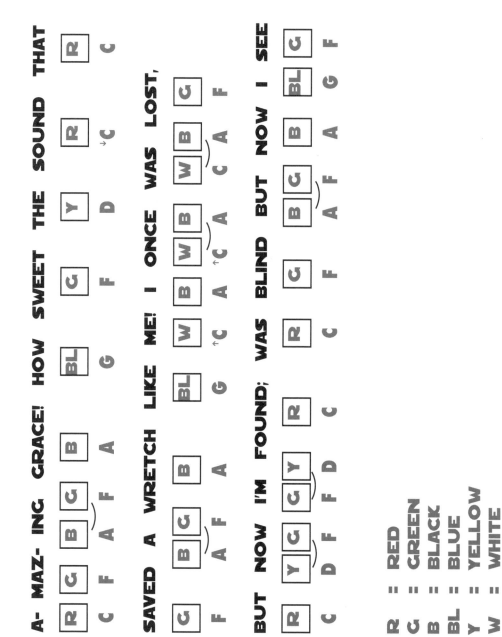

A- MAZ- ING GRACE! HOW SWEET THE SOUND THAT

| R | G | B | BL | | B | G | Y | R | R |
| C | F | A | F | | A | G | F | D | →C | C |

SAVED A WRETCH LIKE ME! I ONCE WAS LOST,

| G | B | B | BL | | W | B | W | B | C |
| F | A | F | A | | G | ↑C | A | C | A | F |

BUT NOW I'M FOUND; WAS BLIND BUT NOW I SEE

| R | Y | G | Y | R | | G | B | BL | G |
| C | D | F | F | D | | C | F | A | G | F |

R = RED
G = GREEN
B = BLACK
BL = BLUE
Y = YELLOW
W = WHITE

'AWAY IN THE MANGER' TONE TUBE SHEET

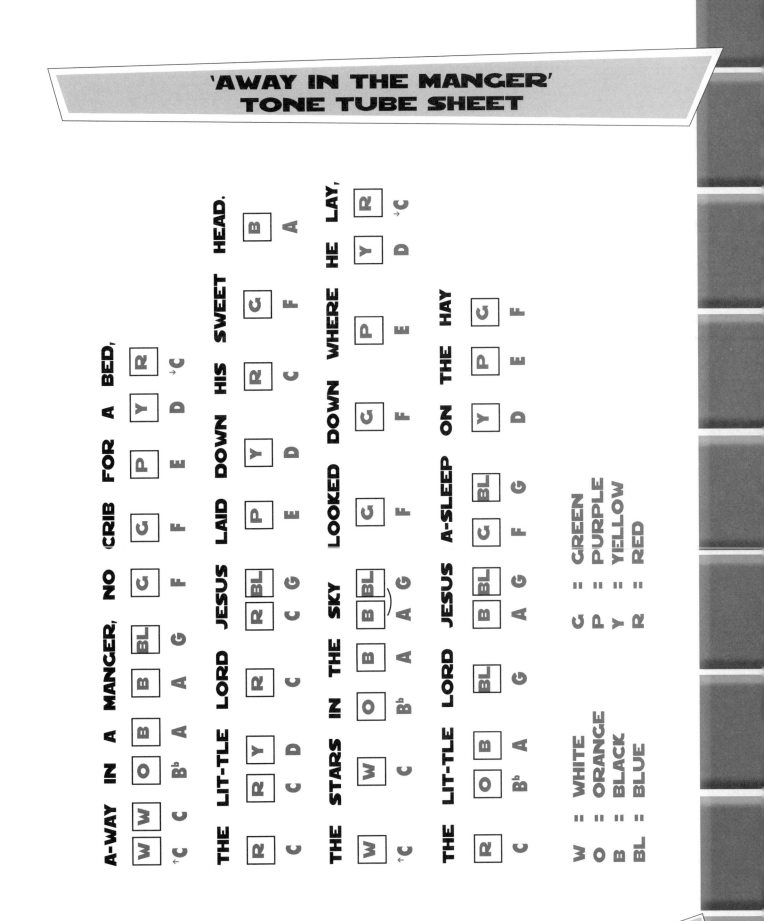

97

'FOR THE BEAUTY OF THE EARTH' TONE TUBE SHEET

FOR THE BEAUTY OF THE EARTH, FOR THE GLORY OF THE SKIES,

G [P][BL]G O O B Y [P] G[Y] [R] R R
F F G F B♭ A D E F D C C C

FOR THE LOVE WHICH FROM OUR BIRTH O-VER AND A-ROUND US LIES;

G [P][BL]G O O B Y[P] [G][Y] [R] R R
F F G F B♭ A D E F D C C C

LORD OF ALL TO THEE WE RAISE THIS OUR HYMM OF

B [BL] G B W O B Y [P] [G] O
A G F A ↑C B♭ A D E F B♭

GRATEFUL PRAISE

B [BL] G
A G F

G = GREEN
P = PURPLE
BL = BLUE
O = ORANGE

B = BLACK
Y = YELLOW
R = RED
W = WHITE

THE SOUND OF SYMBOLS

Use body percussion or rhythm instruments.

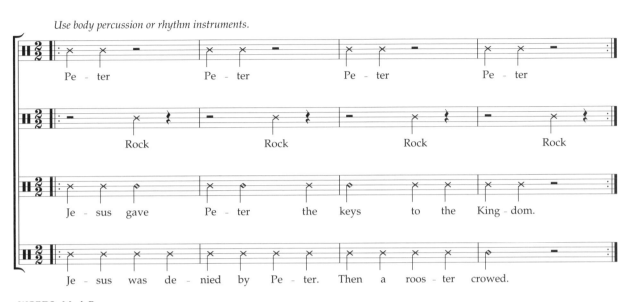

WORDS: Mark Burrows
MUSIC: Mark Burrows

RHYTMN OF RESPECT

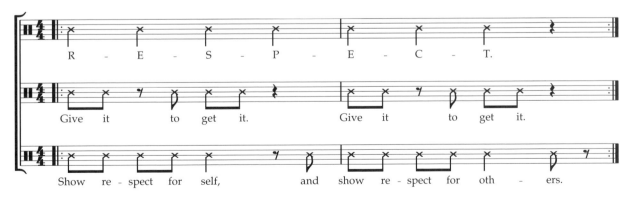

WORDS: Mark Burrows
MUSIC: Mark Burrows

PALM SUNDAY PERCUSSION JAM

1. Big Drum (Congo, Djembe)

Je - sus rode on a don - key's back.

2. Small Drum (frame drum)

Wave the palm branch - es in the air.

3. Rattle or Sandblocks

Peace in heav - en and glo - ry in the high - est.

4. Tambourine

Sing Ho - san - na. Sing Ho - san - na. Sing Ho - san - na. Sing Ho - san - na.

(3.) Optional Rattle part

Peace in heav - en. Peace in heav - en.

Start with part 1 for four measures. Then add part 2 for four measures., and so on. Let the piece grow louder once all the parts have entered. Then end all together on the downbeat of the first measure.

WORDS: Mark Burrows
MUSIC: Mark Burrows

COMMUNION DRUM CIRCLE

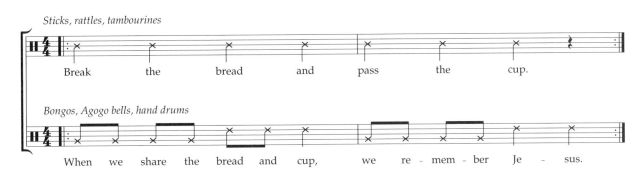

Sticks, rattles, tambourines

Break the bread and pass the cup.

Bongos, Agogo bells, hand drums

When we share the bread and cup, we re-mem-ber Je-sus.

Body percussion can be used in place of instruments. The kids can make new rhythms based on phrases about shared experiences that bring us together.

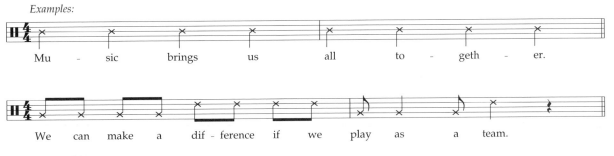

Examples:

Mu - sic brings us all to - geth - er.

We can make a dif - ference if we play as a team.

WORDS: Mark Burrows
MUSIC: Mark Burrows

HOLY SPIRIT

WORDS: Mark Burrows
MUSIC: Mark Burrows

A STORY WITH A BEAT - DANIEL IN THE LION'S DEN

Bongos

Dan - iel was friends with the king.

Claves

Some men were jeal - ous.

Maracas

Dan - iel praised God three times each day.

Agogo Bells

They threw Dan - iel in the den of li - ons.

Guiro

God kept the li - ons from hurt - ing Dan - iel.

WORDS: Mark Burrows
MUSIC: Mark Burrows

THE TEN COMMANDMENTS

(1) "You shall have no gods be - fore me."

(2) Do not make or wor - ship i - dols.

(9) Al - ways try to tell the truth.

(8) You shall not steal. (6) You shall not kill.

(10) Do not cov - et what be - longs to oth - ers.

mem - ber the Sab - bath day to keep it ho - ly. (4) Re -

(5) Hon - or your moth - er. Hon - or your fa - ther.

(3) Do not take the Lord's name in vain.

(7) Al - ways be faith - ful to the ones you love.

The commandments are ordered here according to the rhythms. Easier rhythms start at the top, more difficult ones at the bottom. The numbers indicate the order of the commandments as they appear in the Bible.

WORDS: Mark Burrows
MUSIC: Mark Burrows

CONSERVATION CONCERT

Large cardboard box

Take care of the world God gave us. Earth!

Aluminum can tapped with pencil

cy - cle. Re - cy - cle. Re - cy - cle. Re - cy - cle. Re - Earth!

Plastic soda bottle rattles

Re - use. Re - use. Re - use. Re - use. Earth!

Cardboard tubes

Care for the plants. Care for the an - i - mals. Earth!

Cardboard shoebox

Bi - o - de - grad - a - ble. That's the way to go! Earth!

WORDS: Mark Burrows
MUSIC: Mark Burrows

STORY SAMBA

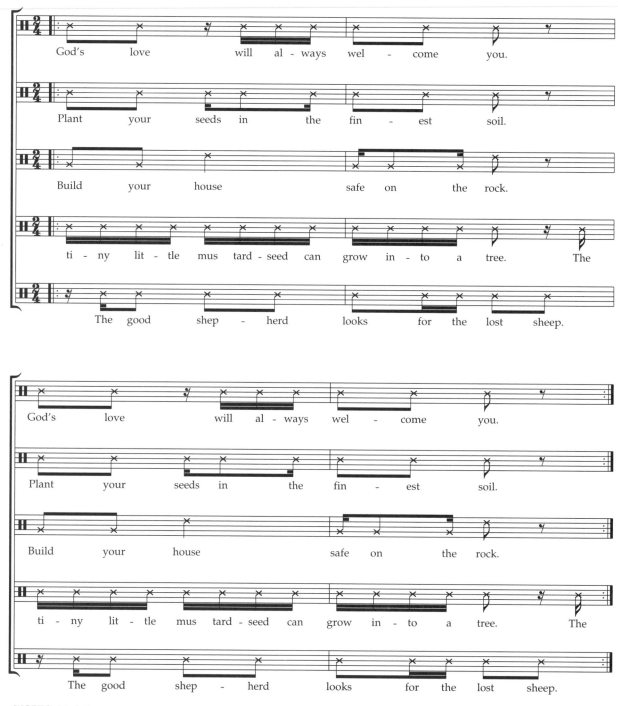

God's love will al - ways wel - come you.

Plant your seeds in the fin - est soil.

Build your house safe on the rock.

ti - ny lit - tle mus tard - seed can grow in - to a tree. The

The good shep - herd looks for the lost sheep.

God's love will al - ways wel - come you.

Plant your seeds in the fin - est soil.

Build your house safe on the rock.

ti - ny lit - tle mus tard - seed can grow in - to a tree. The

The good shep - herd looks for the lost sheep.

WORDS: Mark Burrows
MUSIC: Mark Burrows

GO FISH

WORDS: Mark Burrows
MUSIC: Mark Burrows

PERCUSSION WITH PROVERBS

WORDS: Mark Burrows
MUSIC: Mark Burrows

INDEX

Accompany a Bible song 88
Agogo bells 27

Bass drums 71
Bottle flutes 25
Balloons 34, 56
Berimbau 63
Boing! 67
Bongos 55
Balloon music 34
Bottle mallets 25
Boy's Lunch, The 79
Bull-roarer 47

Call and response 86
Castanets 15
Clip clop hooves 23
Chajchas 24
Claves/rhythm sticks 71
Create a musical sound effects story 89
Crickets 25
Comb cricket 67
Compose a Soundtrack 84
Conventional Didgeridoo 1 43
Conventional Didgeridoo 2 44
Cuica 41
Cup hooves 67

Daniel in the Lions' Den 91
Didgeridoos
  Conventional Didgeridoo 1 43
  Conventional Didgeridoo 2 44
  Slide Didgeridoo 45
Djembe 65
Doumbek 57
Drums 53
  Bass drums 71
  Bongos 55
  Djembe 65
  Doumbek 57
  Drums in the Bible 53
  Ocean drums 20
  Peter Yes-and-No Drum 36

Small hand drum 54

Esther's story 68

Go Fish! 87
God the Great Musician 82
Guiro 20
Guitar, one-string 70

Harp 61
Harp pattern 94

Incidental music 80
Integrating instrument-making
  into a lesson 7

Jesus Calms the Story 81

Kalimba 49
Kazoo 68
Kazooka 51

Making instruments, making choices 6
Making music in the classroom 73
Maracas 23
Musical rebus story 68
Music sheets 95
  Amazing Grace 96
  Away in a Manger 97
  For the Beauty of the Earth 98
  Joyful, Joyful, We Adore Thee 95

Nessie 46

Ocean drums 17
One-string guitar 70

Patterns
  Bull-roarer 93
  Harp 109
Percussion Instruments
  Agogo bells 28
  Bass drums 71

Bongos 55
Bottle mallets 25
Castanets 15
Chajchas 25
Claves/rhythm sticks 71
Clip clop hooves 24
Crickets 26
Djembe 65
Doumbek 57
Guiro 22
Human body 7
Maracas 22
Ocean drums 20
Peter yes-and-no drum 36
Rainsticks 21
Shake-o-saurus 32
Shekeres 30
Sistrum 19
Small hand drum 54
Tambourine 63
Panpipes 32
Percussion jams 76
Peter's story 37
Peter Yes-and-No Drum 35
Poetry
Ark Was Really Rockin', The 43
Christ in the Stranger's Guise 10
Tone poems 78

Quack! 68

Rain 67
Recyclables, collecting 15
Reinforce a Speech Percussion Piece 89
Recyclables, using to make instruments 14
Rhythm sticks/claves 71
Rhythmic passing games 74
Pass the steady beat 74
Pattern pass 74
Rainsticks 18

Shake-o-saurus 31
Shekeres 29
Sistrum 16
Slide Didgeridoo 45
Small hand drum 54
Soda bottle shofar 14
Soda bottle symphony 26

Sound effects 67
boing! 67
comb cricket 67
cup hooves 67
quack! 68
rain 67
Stories
Boy's Lunch, The 79
Daniel in the Lions' Den 91
Esther's Story 68
Go Fish! 87
God the Great Musician 82
Jesus Calms the Storm 81
Musical rebus story 68, 89
Peter's Story 37
Soda bottle symphony 27
Zacchaeus 8
Story With a Beat, A 90
Stringed instruments 61
Berimbau 63
Guitar, one-string 70
Harp 59

Tambourine 59
Tell a Story Using Body Percussion 9
Tone Poem 78
Tone Tubes 38

Using the body as an instrument
Percussion sounds 8
Mouth sounds 11

Wind instruments
Conventional Didgeridoo 1 44
Conventional Didgeridoo 2 45
Bottle flutes 26
Kazoo 68
Kazooka 52
Nessie 46
Panpipes 33
Slide Didgeridoo 45
Soda bottle shofar 17

NOTES